D1440764

INSTINCT
PUTTING

INSTINCT PUTTING

Putt Your Best Using the
Breakthrough, Science-Based
Target Vision Putting Technique

Cary Heath, Ph.D.
Bob Christina, Ph.D.
Eric Alpenfels

GOTHAM
BOOKS

GOTHAM BOOKS
Published by Penguin Group (USA) Inc.
375 Hudson Street, New York, New York 10014, U.S.A.
Penguin Group (Canada), 90 Eglinton Avenue East, Suite 700, Toronto, Ontario
M4P 2Y3, Canada (a division of Pearson Penguin Canada Inc.); Penguin Books
Ltd, 80 Strand, London WC2R 0RL, England; Penguin Ireland, 25 St Stephen's
Green, Dublin 2, Ireland (a division of Penguin Books Ltd); Penguin Group
(Australia), 250 Camberwell Road, Camberwell, Victoria 3124, Australia (a di-
vision of Pearson Australia Group Pty Ltd); Penguin Books India Pvt Ltd, 11
Community Centre, Panchsheel Park, New Delhi – 110 017, India; Penguin
Group (NZ), 67 Apollo Drive, Rosedale, North Shore 0632, New Zealand (a di-
vision of Pearson New Zealand Ltd); Penguin Books (South Africa) (Pty) Ltd, 24
Sturdee Avenue, Rosebank, Johannesburg 2196, South Africa

Penguin Books Ltd, Registered Offices: 80 Strand, London WC2R 0RL, England

Published by Gotham Books, a member of Penguin Group (USA) Inc.

First printing, August 2008
10 9 8 7 6 5 4 3 2 1

LIBRARY OF CONGRESS CATALOGING-IN-PUBLICATION DATA
Heath, Cary.
    Instinct putting: putt your best using the breakthrough, science-based
target vision putting technique / Cary Heath, Bob Christina, Eric Alpenfels.
        p.   cm.
    ISBN 978-1-592-40353-0 (hardcover) 1. Putting (Golf) I. Christina,
Bob. II. Alpenfels, Eric. III. Title.
    GV979.P8H43 2008
    796.352'35—dc22   2007045994

Printed in the United States of America
Set in Trump Mediaeval with PMN Caecilia • Designed by Sabrina Bowers

While the author has made every effort to provide accurate telephone numbers
and Internet addresses at the time of publication, neither the publisher nor the
author assumes any responsibility for errors, or for changes that occur after
publication. Further, the publisher does not have any control over and does not
assume any responsibility for author or third-party Web sites or their content.

Contents

Bob Christina:
To my loving wife, Barbara, for her undying support of my passion for studying the most effective ways to teach, learn, and play the game of golf

Eric Alpenfels:
To my loving wife and life partner Anita, for her continual support and encouragement to pursue my dreams

Cary Heath:
For Dad, and for Tanner

Introduction

You say you want a revolution . . .
You say you've got a real solution . . .
Well, you know
We'd all love to see the plan.

—John Lennon

I'll do almost anything to make a putt drop.

—Jack Nicklaus

Putting is far and away the most important single element in playing the game of golf. Here's why: On a par-72 course, an even-par round typically calls for fourteen tee shots with the driver, four tee shots with an iron on par-3 holes, four shots with woods from the fairway on long par-5 holes, fourteen iron shots to the green, and thirty-six putts. *Therefore, putting accounts for fully half the strokes in a typical round of golf—as many shots as the rest of the game combined.* It stands to reason that the single most important thing you can do to improve your golf *score* is to become a better putter.

14 DRIVER SHOTS
4 FAIRWAY WOODS
4 PAR 3 IRONS
14 IRONS TO GREEN
36 + 36 = 72
36 PUTTS

Putting accounts for half the strokes in a typical round of golf.

This book will help you to do exactly that—step by step, from the practice green to the course. Unlike other golf instruction books, which merely tweak this or modify that—but offer little that is really new—this book presents an entirely different *paradigm*. We call this paradigm *Instinct Putting*. The intent of this book is to impart a clear understanding of *Instinct Putting* ("IP" for short), and guide you in adopting IP for your own game through a unique and enjoyable program of practice drills and exercises.

The IP method represents a revolutionary departure from conventional wisdom. However, it does not require radical changes in the mechanics of your putting stroke. IP allows you to go on putting pretty much as you always have, except for one all-important difference: **You will execute the putt while looking at the target rather than the ball.** In conventional putting, one is taught to look at the ball for the duration of the putting stroke, and not to look up until the ball is well on its way to the hole. In the alternative paradigm—IP—one looks at the hole or a point along the target line, not the ball, throughout the putting stroke.

Instinct putting requires that you focus both visually *and mentally* on the target—that you

really cast your consciousness out to the place
where you intend to
leave the ball. You
will find that
when you
do this, when
you focus inten-
sely on the target,
you will not be able
to think much about
the mechanics of the
putting stroke. The
brain can handle mul-
tiple tasks subcon-
sciously, but it is
relatively lim-
ited in terms
of conscious thought. As
you focus consciously on the target, your brain
will process a steady stream of visual information regarding the position of the target and the
length of the putt. But your brain cannot do this
and consciously "think through" the mechanics
of the putting stroke at the same time. Fortu-
nately, it doesn't have to.

Each of us is endowed by nature with a powerful subconscious "athletic intuition." We rely on it all the time. Imagine how difficult walking would be (not to mention gymnastics or ballet) if you tried to think consciously about where to

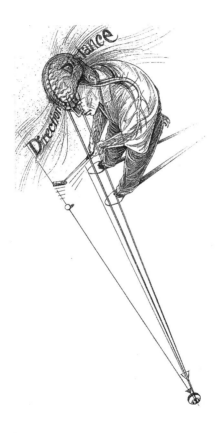

place each foot, how to shift your weight forward, and what to do with your arms. A complete description of the simple act of walking, in full anatomical and physiological detail, would fill hundreds of pages of text. Yet we are able to walk with ease, and perform other complicated physical acts every day, precisely because we direct our attention away from the action itself and focus instead on the destination. We think about *where* to walk, not *how*. And so it is with putting. **Your skill would improve dramatically if you learned to concentrate on WHERE to putt the ball and didn't try to think so much about HOW to execute the stroke.** That is exactly what this book is all about—a radically unorthodox putting method in which one focuses on *where* to putt the ball, not *how* to execute the stroke.

If you thought this book was going to be all about the mechanics of putting, then you are in for a surprise. Some very knowledgeable people have written excellent putting instruction books that deal with mechanics, if that's what you're looking for. This just isn't one of those books. We take putting in a very different direction. It runs against the grain of accepted thought, and for that reason it will be read with much skepticism by some. Golf is essentially a conservative game, guided strongly by tradition, respectful of time-tested fundamentals, reluctant to accept departures from conventional wisdom. Although there are exceptions—PGA Hall of Fame golfer Johnny Miller, for example, stands "outside the box" with much of his analysis and instruction—it seems fair to say that truly creative thinkers in golf are the exceptions that prove the rule.

On the other hand, this traditionalist generalization of golf might not be entirely accurate when it comes to putting. Touring professionals and weekend amateurs alike will agree that putting is the most subjective and most individualistic aspect of the game of golf. Good players have remarkably similar full-shot swings, especially through the so-called "hitting area." At the crucial moment of impact they are doing about the same thing with the club. But when it comes to the art of putting—and putting is an art—their styles may vary considerably. Perhaps the reason for so much diversity in putting styles lies in the fact that mechanical efficiency and physical strength are much less important than "touch" in this department of the game. And because touch is such a subjective thing, different people are going to capture it in their own, individual ways.

While it may be very subjective, touch is not magic, nor is it given only to a chosen few. Any person of average athletic ability can learn to capture that seemingly elusive feeling on virtually every putt. This book will teach you how.

THIS LEARNING PROCESS INVOLVES THREE GENERAL PHASES:

1. Presenting the mind with a complete and thorough understanding of IP—*how* it works, scientific evidence that in fact it *does* work, and a thorough explanation of *why* it works.

2. Practicing a set of *skill development* drills that trains the body to perform what the mind understands. In this phase our mind gradually gives up more and more conscious control of the movements involved in performing the action. Conscious thinking begins to give way to intuition.

3. Practicing a set of drills that facilitates the *transfer* of IP from the practice green to actual play on the course, including competitive situations. In this phase of learning you become so skillful that athletic intuition, rather than conscious thought, controls the putting action.

The material in this book is organized generally along these same lines. **Part One,** "Understanding Instinct Putting," comprises three chapters that are devoted to imparting a solid understanding of IP. **Part Two,** "Learning Instinct Putting," presents drills that will guide you through the development of IP skills, and then the transference of those skills to actual play on the course.

If putting is the most subjective part of golf, it is also the most frustrating. Most of us can accept the fact that we lack the strength and coordination to hit drives as far as John Daly, or reach long par-5s with anything like the regularity of Davis Love III. But are we so inferior when it comes to a twenty-foot putt? Taking three to get down from twenty feet really galls us because we know that we are physically capable of doing much better. We should be as good on the greens as Tiger Woods! (Well, almost.) To use an analogy, we can accept the impossibility of equaling concert pianist Van Cliburn's perform-ance of the *Brandenburg Concerti*; it is simply and obviously beyond the reach of our abilities. But our rendition of "Chopsticks" might be fairly comparable to his. In other words, one need not possess the exceptional talents of a Tiger Woods to achieve a reasonable measure of success in this aspect of the game. A little athletic intuition—if you'll just trust it—will suffice. Be-fore we go any further, let's look a little deeper into what we mean by "athletic intuition."

Johnny Miller, and the renowned teaching pro-fessional Phil Galvano, Sr. both articu-lated the es-sence of

Release the Tiger within

athletic intuition well, and it pays to repeat here what they had to say. Two quotations are especially incisive: Miller wrote that "Conscious thought is inhibiting. . . . During the physical act of stroking the ball, *I'm conscious of nothing and aware of everything*." And Galvano, in a passage informed by Zen philosophy, states that "if [the golf swing] acts, it must act *by itself* without mental or physical interference." What did they mean?

Consider a quarterback throwing a football. He doesn't try to calculate where to throw the ball, even though the perfect trajectory and speed could be calculated mathematically, given data on all the relevant factors such as wind, the speed and direction of the receiver, and so on. The quarterback is *aware* of these factors, but he releases the ball *instinctively*, with virtually no "conscious thought" about the myriad elements involved. That is what Miller meant by being "conscious of nothing and aware of everything." Actually, the same is true for all other situations in which we perform complicated physical acts totally instinctively, from playing the piano to riding a bicycle to signing our names. We rely upon a process that is mental, and yet "thoughtless" in terms of consciously thinking your way through what you're trying to do.

Conscious of nothing . . . aware of everything

At the very highest level of athletic perfor-mance, pure athletic intuition acts completely unimpeded by conscious thought. When you per-form at this most instinctive level, you don't have the feeling that you are "forcing things to hap-pen." You're simply *allowing* your body to do what it knows how to do—*instinctively.* Galvano meant precisely that when he wrote that the golf swing "must act *by itself* without mental or physical in-terference."

You might be wondering if *Instinct Putting* was inspired by Zen Buddhism, with all the talk about the subconscious mind and athletic intui-tion. Actually, both the title and the central premise owe more to "Lucky" McDaniel than to the Buddha. In a book entitled *Instinct Shooting*, Mike Jennings told the story of one Lamar "Lucky" McDaniel, who made an international reputation for himself in the 1950s with an amazing method of teaching people of all ages and athletic abilities to shoot clay pigeons. Lucky's method of shooting was entirely instinctive—and as natural as point-ing your finger at the target. His instruction was simple: You don't want to look at the gun, the barrel or sights, but at the target. He taught his students to look at what they were trying to hit, as intensely as they could, until they couldn't think about or even see anything else. After just a few practice shots, his students would begin hitting the target with amazing consistency. They quickly became "instinct shooters."

Considered radical when *Instinct Shooting* was first published in 1959, his method is now widely used in bird hunting, skeet shooting—whenever you're trying to hit a moving target with a shotgun. Even police departments and the military have taught instinct shooting as a quick-draw-and-shoot technique for emergency situations. As you will soon discover, the method of putting described in *Instinct Putting* is equally instinctive, equally natural, and equally effective for anyone willing to give it a serious try. This book will undoubtedly seem every bit as radical as *Instinct Shooting* did when it was first published. IP not only goes against centuries of conventional wisdom in golf, it violates a bedrock principle of every "stick and ball" type of sport: "Keep your eye on the ball."

Instinct Putting is not a book for those who refuse to consider new ideas. A cautious skepticism is reasonable, but obstinacy closes the door to the possibility of positive change. Nor is this a book for "small thinkers." Small thinking leads to mini-thinking, which leads to hardly thinking at all. Let us bid farewell to those who are unwilling or unable to change, and wish them a happy deliverance from their putting woes.

Instinct Putting is a book for those who are thoughtfully open-minded, who can envision what could be, not just what is and always has been. Does that sound a bit like you? If so, then we invite you to take an extraordinary journey to better golf. It is a journey both of escape and of discovery. For only when you escape the old ideas that distract, confuse, and inhibit can you discover the natural athlete—the instinct putter—within yourself.

Do you want to know the real solution? Do you want to see the plan? Give IP a try. You stand a very good chance of putting better than you ever have.

Look at the target, not the ball. Not exactly conventional wisdom, is it? Welcome to the revolution.

PART ONE

UNDERSTANDING INSTINCT PUTTING

Chapter 1

Is Instinct Putting for You?

> The difficulty lies not in the new ideas, but in escaping from the old ones.
>
> —John Maynard Keynes

We all have flaws in our putting technique, some more detrimental than others. If you tend to make certain mistakes over and over, you are definitely a candidate for IP. First, answer each of the following eight questions. Your score will indicate whether or not you are a candidate for IP.

- Do you typically three-putt more than twice per round?

- Do you often leave yourself a putt of more than three feet after stroking a mid- to long-distance putt?

- Do you tend to lose your "feel" for the putt after you've addressed the ball?

- Do you have a tendency to decelerate the putter and not stroke through the ball smoothly?

- Do you sometimes peek or look up too soon on your putts?

- Does seeing the movement of your putterhead and shaft and your hands and arms during your stroke distract you from making a good putt or cause you to try to consciously control the stroke?

- Do you have difficulty stroking the ball on your intended line?

- Do you have difficulty maintaining a steady posture—in other words, keeping "still"—during your putting stroke?

Now it's time to score yourself. If you answered "yes" this many times . . .

0: **You are among the greatest putters on the planet** and not a candidate for IP. *You* should teach *us* how to putt.

1–2: **You are a good putter** and possibly a candidate for IP. We suggest that you practice IP to see if it helps you eliminate or reduce the frequency of the one or two putting flaws that you have. If it does, then we recommend that you give serious consideration to using IP when you play.

3–4: **You are a putter in need of some help** and definitely a candidate for IP. We propose that you practice IP to see if it helps with the three or four putting flaws that you have. If it does, we recommend that you learn to use IP when you play.

5+: **You are a putter in need of substantial help** and definitely a candidate for IP. You should practice IP with the expectation that you will eventually use it when you play.

THE TOSS TEST

Now let's move on to the Toss Test. You are about to get an initial taste of what IP is all about. It is best to do this exercise on a practice green, but if your floor covering is suitable or you have a putting practice mat, you can do this test at home as well. Place a ball on the putting surface about twenty-five to thirty-five feet from the hole (or other target if you're not on a putting green). Hold another ball in your hand. Address the ball on the ground in a posture similar to your normal putting stance, but without your putter in hand. You should be standing with your feet and shoulders more or less parallel to the target line. Turn your head to look naturally at the target and toss the ball you are holding toward the hole. *Try to sink it as you would a putt—not "on the fly," of course, but with a bowling action.* If you putt right-handed, then your left arm is closer to the target and you'll be tossing the ball with your right hand. (It would be just the opposite, of course, if you putt left-handed.)

Make several tosses from this position. Turn your head so that you can clearly see the target, but do not open your shoulders any more than you would if you were putting the ball. Pay particular attention to distance control. Repeat this exercise enough times to establish a pattern around the hole—at least half a dozen balls. You'll probably see that distance control, not direction, is the more challenging aspect of the drill. We all tend to think that a putt is good if it passes near the hole, if it is on line. What matters, of course, is where the ball finishes. We'll have more to say about this. For now, just work on distance control. After a while, you'll begin to "feel" the proper amount of strength to apply to the toss.

Now let's change the routine just a bit. Assume your address position and prepare to toss the ball again. But this time, before you execute the toss, look away from the target and focus instead on the ball that you've placed on the ground by your feet, as you normally do when putting. With your eyes focused on that ball, toss the other ball to the target. How well did you do? If you're like most, you will immediately sense that you've lost some of your "feel" for distance, and probably for the line of the toss as well. In fact, golfers have told us that the moment they looked down at the ball instead of at the hole, they completely understood the essence of instinct putting.

Perform the Toss Test from various distances and, if you're on an actual green, from different directions with different breaks, or "borrow." With successive tosses, alternate between looking at the target as you toss and at the ball you've placed in putting position on the ground. You'll find that you have much better "feel," especially

The Toss Test

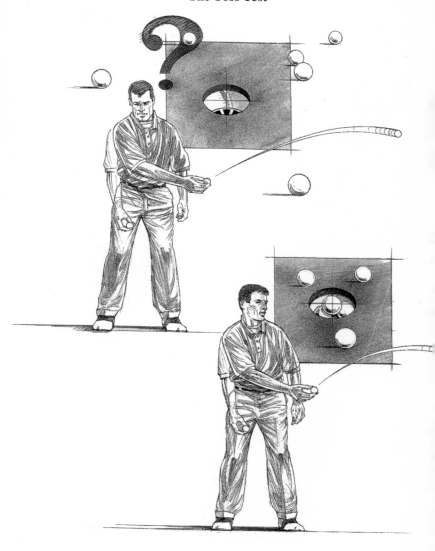

for distance, when you focus your eyes and your attention on the target. (Understand that you are still tossing the ball at this point—no putters yet.) You will be amazed at how much better your distance control soon becomes when you look at the hole instead of the ball.

You should not be surprised in the least to discover that looking at the target gives better results than looking down at the ball. After all, is it not so in most other sports? Imagine how difficult it would be to make a free throw in basketball if you looked at the line instead of the basket as you executed the shot. No quarterback in football would attempt a pass while staring at a spot on the ground near his feet—in effect, what conventional putting requires the golfer to do when putting. Try hitting the bull's-eye on a dartboard with your eyes fixed firmly on the floor. It's next to impossible. At this point you are probably thinking, Okay, you're right about throwing a ball or a dart—*but that isn't putting!* Putting means striking a ball with a stick, and you most assuredly *do* have to look at a ball to hit it squarely with a stick. After all, you wouldn't advise tennis players to keep their eyes focused on the net, would you? Are baseball players taught to keep their eyes fixed firmly on the center field wall? Of course not.

The most common concern about instinct putting is that one can't strike the ball solidly without looking at it throughout the putting stroke. This concern is entirely reasonable—and it is also dead wrong.

The tennis and baseball analogies are not quite correct, because baseballs and tennis balls are in motion as one attempts to hit them. *But the golf ball is perfectly still until it is struck.* The physical relationship of the ball to the player is fixed at address, and it doesn't change until the putter contacts the ball.

In this respect, putting is more closely analogous to typing, or playing a musical instrument, than to hitting the ball in other stick-and-ball games. Consider the pianist, who confidently strikes precisely the intended key—*with eyes focused on a sheet of musical notation, not the keyboard* (or the fingers that dance upon it). Finding a specific key among the eighty-eight that comprise a standard keyboard is possible because the spatial relationship of the piano keys to the musician is *fixed*—the keys aren't moving through space, as a baseball that has been thrown or a tennis ball that has been swatted are. Furthermore, that spatial relationship is *constant*. That is, the keys are positioned the same way, every time, on every piano.

It is very much the same with IP. The spatial relationship of the ball to you, the golfer, is *fixed*. And if you set up to every putt consistently—the same way, every time, on every putt—the relationship will also be *constant*. Then you will be able to contact the ball solidly while looking at the target, just as the pianist is able to strike all the right keys while looking away from the keyboard. This is not just theoretical, either. As you will see in Chapter 2, *tests have shown that golfers learn this aspect of IP—how to strike the ball squarely, consistently, and instinctively while looking at the target—in as few as forty-five putts.*

We will return to the question of why IP works (and to the piano analogy, as well), but first we need to establish the fact that *it does work*. As any good scientist will tell you, what sounds like a good idea might not work in practice. We'll review various sources of evidence including a study conducted by two of the authors of *Instinct Putting* (Bob Christina and Eric Alpenfels) who analyzed literally thousands of putts. What they discovered was nothing short of astonishing. The next chapter takes a close look at this evidence. Does IP really work? The proof, as they say, is in the pudding—or the *putting*, in this case.

Chapter 2

The Evidence

> I come from a country that raises corn
> and cotton and cockleburs and
> Democrats, and frothy eloquence neither
> convinces nor satisfies me. I'm from Missouri.
> You've got to show me.
> —Former Missouri Congressman
> Willard D. Vandiver

Now that you have been introduced to IP and have an idea of how it is supposed to work, the next question is, what evidence exists to indicate that the method can actually improve your putting performance? It's a fair question, even for those who have already decided to give IP a try. And frankly, we would not expect you to invest a lot of time and energy in learning a new technique without solid reason to believe that your efforts will be rewarded. You'll see that numerous sources of evidence establish the conclusion that IP really does work. It is more than just an interesting possibility—we'll show you.

Your authors did not invent instinct putting, although we did coin that term for it. Nor were we the first to attempt to validate its effectiveness. The story of IP actually goes back many years, and to the best of our knowledge the concept originated in—where else?—the British Isles.

In 1973, a *Golf Digest* book entitled *All About Putting* reported that an Englishman named Hunter Diack had conducted a couple of practical tests to see how well he putted with two different methods: the orthodox method of putting while looking at the ball, and a new method that required him to look at the hole instead of the ball. Diack tested himself by putting to holes that were 2¾ inches in diameter (a regulation hole is 4¼ inches in diameter), and from a distance of between seven and eight feet.

The test comprised a total of 1,000 putts—500 while looking at the hole and 500 while looking at the ball. Diack stroked ten putts using one method and then ten putts with the other. He continued switching back and forth in this manner until he had struck 500 putts each way. He found that he sank 40 percent of the putts while looking at the hole and 35 percent while looking at the ball. The constant alternating between methods had an unsettling effect, so he decided to stroke an additional 200 putts, this time performing one hundred successive putts while looking at the hole and the same number while looking at the ball. In this experiment he sank fifty-four putts while looking at the hole and only thirty-nine while looking at the ball. **Taken together, the data clearly indicated that Diack putted better when he looked at the hole than when he looked at the ball.** These findings are not conclusive, however, because the tests were not scientifically sound, a point to which we shall return shortly. Still, his results are quite remarkable given that he had spent his entire golfing life to that point—some fifty years—as an orthodox putter.

Diack never completely abandoned the orthodox style despite his own evidence that looking at the target was somewhat more effective. He alternately used both methods, orthodox and IP, with confidence and success for the rest of his golfing days. He also employed both methods on the practice green, for a couple of reasons. First, he felt that switching from one method to the other broke the monotony of always practicing the same way.

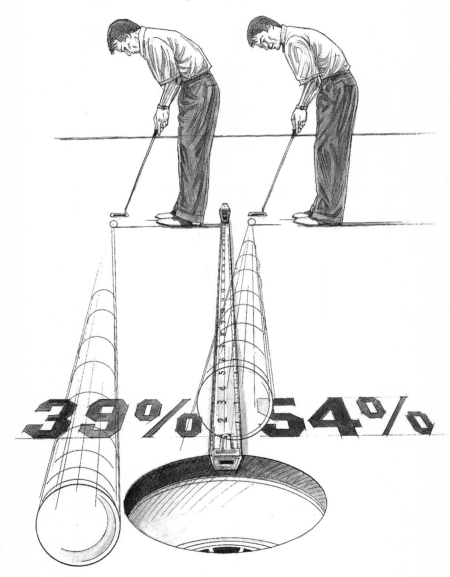

Diack sank more putts when he looked at the hole.

And second, he discovered that after practicing his new method, he was no longer distracted by the movement of the putterhead, a persistent problem when he putted while looking at the ball. In other words, he discovered that *practicing IP improved his orthodox putting as well.* It is an intriguing idea, and if correct, it could change the way all golfers practice their putting, including those who choose to stay with the orthodox, look-at-the-ball method for actual play on the course.

Diack's tests were not very solid as a matter of scientific method, for a number of reasons: Only one person was tested, rather than a number of people; the tester and the subject were the same person, which makes it impossible to know the extent to which his own biases were controlled; only one relatively short putting distance was tested, rather than a wide range of putting distances; and the diameter of the hole was considerably smaller than regulation. Nonetheless, Diack's experiences with IP clearly suggest two hypotheses that can be scientifically tested:

- Looking at the hole while executing the putt is a more effective method of *putting* than looking at the ball while executing the stroke, and

- Looking at the hole is an effective training drill, a useful method of *practicing* in order to improve proficiency at conventional putting.

It would be left to others to conduct proper scientific tests of these hypotheses, and this is where Bob Christina and Eric Alpenfels come into the story of instinct putting. They initially looked at Diack's second proposition, that skills developed from practicing while looking at the hole transfer positively to improve putting while looking at the ball.

To test this idea, they conducted a study in 2002 at the Pinehurst Golf Academy (where Alpenfels is the director) and published their results one year later in the March issue of *Golf Magazine*. They instructed experienced adult amateur male and female golfers to practice stroking forty long putts (twenty to forty feet) in a random order while looking at the hole, not the ball. However, they pre- and post-tested the participants on a different set of putts (twenty-three to forty-three feet) as they putted *using their own method of looking at the ball*. The study revealed that, after practicing putting while looking at the hole, golfers who returned to their own putting method of looking at the ball in the post-test significantly reduced their average putting error by nine inches in just one short training session. Hunter Diack was right! **This finding clearly indicates that practicing putting while looking at the hole has considerable potential as a drill to improve one's distance control on long putts, even when the golfer putts by looking at the ball in actual play.**

Based on this evidence, Christina and Alpenfels began teaching IP *as a practice drill* to interested golfers in the Pinehurst Golf Academy. Time after time they observed students rapidly becoming better orthodox putters, especially in terms of distance control. The researchers began to wonder: If putting while looking at the hole worked so well as a *practice drill* (Diack's second hypothesis), would students do well to adopt the method as their *regular style of putting* (Diack's first hypothesis)? Is IP simply the more effective method? Was Hunter Diack right about that as well?

In an effort to find out, Christina and Alpenfels followed up their first investigation with another study at the Pinehurst Golf Advantage School, this time focusing on Diack's first proposition.

This study also was published in *Golf Magazine* (October 2005). Here is how the testing was conducted:

- Forty experienced golfers ranging in handicap from eight to thirty-six were randomly assigned to two groups of twenty per group, with the restriction that both groups be balanced in terms of handicap and gender. One group looked at the hole when putting and the other group looked at the ball. All forty golfers used the conventional method of putting, in which they looked at the ball during the stroke.

- Both groups were pretested looking at the ball while putting and then pretested again with one group looking at the ball and the other looking at the hole. The first pretest was given to determine the putting-performance level of each group at the start of the study. The second pretest, or *transfer* test, was given to determine the effect of *switching* from looking at the ball to looking at the hole.

- On both pretests, golfers putted one ball in a random order to each of nine holes, ranging in distance from three to forty-three feet.

- Each group practiced forty-five putts to nine different holes ranging in distance from five to forty-five feet. These nine distances were different from the nine that were used for the pre- and post-tests.

- Each group was post-tested the same way as the second pretest.

- Golfers went through their pre-shot routine and putted as though they were playing medal play.

It should be said that Christina and Alpenfels began their investigation as skeptics. They assumed that the conventional wisdom—that one should always look at the ball when putting in actual play—was still correct, despite what they had learned about IP as a practice drill. They were surprised, to say the least, at what they discovered. **Unambiguously, the results established that after a short training session of only forty-five practice putts looking at the hole or a target, experienced amateur male and female golfers of different handicap levels significantly improved their putting performance, especially on long putts**. In fact, the findings were so dramatic that *Golf Magazine* described them as "amazing" and "shocking." We present the numbers here. You can choose your own best words to describe them.

- On average, on putts that were between twenty-eight and thirty-eight feet in length, the experimental group (those who looked at the hole) had just less than twenty-eight inches remaining to the cup. By contrast, on the same long putts, the control group (those who looked at the ball) left the ball some thirty-seven inches from the hole. That means the experimental group got their putts 24 percent closer, nine inches that can transform an automatic two-putt into a "knee-knocker" to save par. **Conclusion: Long putts finish closer to the hole when you look at the hole instead of the ball.**

- On putts between three feet and eight feet, the experimental group left an average of just under nine inches to the hole, while the control group finished 12.5 inches away. Strictly speaking, the difference is not statistically significant, but those results are not exactly meaningless, either. An extra foot of

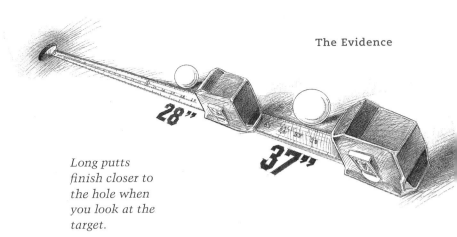

Long putts finish closer to the hole when you look at the target.

"leave" can be the difference between a routine tap-in and the occasional short miss. **Conclusion: Looking at the hole may be more effective on short putts, too.**

• Before switching to looking at the hole, both the experimental group and the control group averaged a leave of about twenty-nine inches on putts from three feet to forty-three feet in original length. After just forty-five putts, the experimental group was leaving the ball only about twenty inches from the hole. That's a 27.5 percent improvement over putts hit while they looked at the ball. But what really matters is this: Those who looked at the hole improved nearly twice as much as those who looked at the ball with the same minimal amount of practice. **Conclusion: Instinct putting is easy to learn.**

- The putting performance of both groups was essentially the same on the first pretest, which was not the case on the second pretest. As expected, the *immediate* effect of switching to looking at the hole caused the putting performance of the experimental group to get worse, on average, by about five inches, while it improved by about five inches for the control group, due to practice. **Conclusion: Improvement comes quickly, but not immediately. Performance may be expected to decline initially before it improves through practice.**

We now know that most players improve remarkably with very little practice at IP. But what about those who have used the method over a considerable period of time? Do they continue to putt successfully with IP, or do they tend to "lose it" and return to orthodox putting? Unfortunately, there is very little information on longtime users, because there have been very few of them. *In-*

stinct putting is the method of the future, not the past. Besides Hunter Diack, who did quite well as an instinct putter for as long as he continued to play golf, we know of only a few golfers who have used the method on a long-term basis. But the method has been used successfully, and we are able briefly to relate the experiences of four golfers who represent a fairly broad spectrum of the golfing population: a former PGA Tour superstar, a current PGA Champions Tour star, a PGA teaching professional, and an average, mid-handicap amateur player.

The first of our players is golfer and popular TV broadcast analyst Johnny Miller. Perhaps you saw Miller playing with his partner and broadcast colleague, Roger Maltbie, against Lanny Wadkins and Gary McCord in a widely viewed, made-for-TV match in 2006, the Golf Channel's *Battle of the Broadcasters.* Much to everyone's surprise, Miller putted while looking at the hole, not the ball, and did so quite successfully. In fact, he made one putt of thirty feet and another of four feet to clinch the match. Miller has struggled through frustrating spells of poor putting on Tour, and has experimented with various grips and putters. When asked about his putting method in the Golf Channel broadcast, he said he was having fun on the greens for the first time in many years.

The second Tour star to use IP is Jim Thorpe. A man of prodigious athletic strength and ability (he played football in college), Thorpe is today a successful and popular player on the PGA Champions Tour. He relies upon IP primarily on lengthy lag putts. As he discussed in a "Playing Lessons from the Pros" segment on the Golf Channel, he feels that looking at the hole or a target point along the line greatly improves his distance control. On shorter putts, Thorpe continues to putt in the orthodox style, because distance control is not as much a problem for him on putts relatively close to the cup.

John Marentette, a PGA teaching professional and low-single-digit handicap player, has been a successful instinct putter since 1994. He began using the method mainly because of poor distance control, especially on mid- to long-distance putts. His problems were actually fairly typical, not just among better players, as he is, but among high-handicappers, as well. Instead of stroking the ball in an easy, natural motion, Marentette found himself focusing almost obsessively on the mechanics of the stroke and what the putterhead was doing at virtually every point throughout the stroke. He sometimes even watched the putter all the way back and through in an attempt to make perfect contact with the ball. He was trying so hard to "manufacture" the perfect stroke that he was incapable of simply putting the ball naturally or instinctively—or accurately.

As he attempted to overcome these problems, Marentette experimented with various regular-length and long putters and many different grips and stances. No matter what he tried, success eluded him. Eventually he returned to his original method of putting, but with one major difference: He looked at the hole (or sometimes a smaller target within the circumference of the hole) rather than the ball throughout the putting stroke. (He even looked at the hole on breaking putts of all lengths.) To his pleasant surprise, Marentette quickly found that looking at the target took his mind off the irrelevant thoughts that were interfering with his own natural ability to produce a serviceable putting stroke. His distance control improved almost immediately.

Encouraged by his initial success, Marentette trained diligently over the next four weeks, several times a week, until he felt ready to try IP in actual play. On the course he again experienced immediate success, first in practice rounds, and soon after in competitive play, as well. He continues to putt successfully using this method and is absolutely convinced that it is superior to the orthodox, look-at-the-ball style of putting. He also enthusiastically recommends the method to his students, especially those who are having difficulty with distance control.

Another longtime instinct putter is amateur golfer Tony Accetta. When he began experimenting with the method, Accetta carried a handicap of sixteen and typically recorded ten to twelve three-putt greens a round. Shortly after he started IP, his handicap dropped by five strokes. Not only did he improve greatly on long putts, but he also consistently made more short putts. In 2006, his handicap got down to a seven. His progress was not steady, however, and it didn't come without a lot of practice.

Accetta first tried IP indoors on a smooth carpet. In the very beginning he felt disoriented and clumsy, but after only a few strokes he began to feel more comfortable and soon was hitting his target consistently—to his own very great surprise! When he tried his new method on a putting green, his first few putts were not very successful. However, he kept at it, and in the weeks and months that followed, he practiced on many different types of practice greens—flat and undulating, fast and slow, grainy and smooth. In time his confidence grew stronger and his proficiency steadily improved.

After a considerable amount of practice, Accetta took his new putting method to the course in actual play. His confidence was tested immediately, as he three-putted several times during that first eighteen-hole round. But all was not bad. He made several good putts in the twelve-foot range and holed a number of short putts. With each round both his distance control and directional accuracy improved, and the number of critical mis-hits greatly diminished.

Finally convinced that his method of putting worked, Accetta wanted to share it with everyone. So in 1994, he authored and published a twenty-six-page monograph titled *Target*

Observation Putting. To our knowledge, it was the only written work devoted entirely to the method before *Instinct Putting.*

We've shown you the facts, so now let's consider the theory that explains them.

Chapter 3

The Explanation

> It works well in practice, but how does it
> sound in theory?
>
> —Old Science Quip

The evidence establishes, beyond question, that IP really does work. Why does IP work so well? What is the theory that explains the facts?

Numbers alone don't tell the whole story. The second Christina-Alpenfels study provided two other observations, in addition to the statistical data, that help to explain why players who looked at the hole improved so much. *First of all, they kept a very steady body posture—kept "still"—throughout the putting stroke.* You hear it all the time on TV: "Look how still Tiger (or Annika, or Vijay, or whoever) stayed through that putt!" If your posture changes while you putt, it becomes much more difficult to make solid contact on the sweet spot of the putterface. Perhaps the fear of whiffing explains it, but the fact is that golfers who looked at the hole instead of the ball maintained their posture much better throughout the stroke. Some people experience a special problem in this regard—they tend to look up early to see where the ball is going. Obviously this problem doesn't exist in a method that *begins* with the head up and eyes focused on where the ball is supposed to go.

A second observation from the Christina-Alpenfels investigation is also very telling. *Those who looked at the hole or target when they putted did not decelerate the putter during the forward part of the stroke to the ball.* Slowing the stroke before impact is a death move in terms of both distance and directional control. When you are unsure about how hard to strike a putt, you tend to slow down the putter just before contact with the ball. Your brain seems to scream at you, "Slam on the brakes!" The result is not just that you tend to decelerate the putter, but that you do so inconsistently from putt to putt, which causes even more uncertainty, and so on. It becomes a vicious cycle that is very difficult to break.

You might also tend to slow your putting stroke when you are unsure about the accuracy of your aim. By slowing down, you feel as though you can better manipulate the putter to start the ball on the proper path to the hole. Ironically, this attempt to control the putter only leads to further directional inaccuracy. Most putters are designed in such a way that the toe does not speed up or slow down quite as fast as the shaft. In slightly more technical terms, a tiny measure of axial rotation of the putterface around the puttershaft inevitably occurs when the speed of the shaft is suddenly changed. As a result, any sudden slowing of the shaft will tend to cause the putterface to close and jeopardize accuracy.

To summarize, the second Christina-Alpenfels study yielded a couple of nonstatistical observations about what golfers do when they look at the hole rather than the ball when putting: They tend to keep a relatively still posture throughout the stroke, and they tend not to decelerate the putter in the forward swing to the ball. These observations are certainly instructive, and most would agree that they identify characteristics shared by all good putters. However, they do not explain the effectiveness of IP *in particular*. If there is something really powerful at work here, something *unique to IP*, what is it?

We offer the following two explanations, which are distinct but very much interrelated. The first has to do with using visual input, rather than memory, to mediate the coordination of muscle and mind in executing the putting stroke. The second has to do with the power of "athletic intuition." It all sounds a bit abstract, we know. But stay with us. This isn't exactly rocket science, either.

In most sports—most activities involving motor skills, in fact—the eyes provide a *continuous visual input* of information to the brain. The brain then translates what both eyes see to give you depth perception and the ability to judge distance, and processes any other visual information relevant to the task at hand. In putting, you achieve this perception of depth and distance when you look at the hole, not the ball. Your eyes provide information about other important factors as well, such as whether you are putting uphill or downhill, with the grain or against it.

Visual input is critical whether you look at the target as you stroke the putt or at the ball. (After all, conventional putting does not mean

*Continuous visual input mediates the interaction of
mind and body.*

wearing a blindfold!) Your eyes provide important
information either way, but there is one all-
important difference: When you putt looking at
the target, *the interaction of your brain and the
muscles of your shoulders, arms, and hands is mediated by a continuous flow of visual information.*

Executing the putting stroke then becomes simply a matter of instinctive hand-eye coordination, similar to that involved in rolling the ball to the target when you took the Toss Test. It is quite a different matter, however, when you look at the ball as you strike the putt. In this case, *the interaction of your brain and muscles is mediated by memory of prior visual input.* When you look at the ball you shut off that visual "feed" of information about where the hole is located, whether you are putting uphill or downhill, with the grain or against it, and the speed and break of the green. Your brain must *remember* all of that information, and with every second that you linger over the ball, you run the risk of not remembering correctly.

In contrast to orthodox putting, IP does not require you to remember much at all, because your eyes provide *a constant flow of information* to the brain. This visual information flow is analogous to electricity flowing to a lightbulb. If the flow is broken for even a moment, the light begins to flicker, and that which it illuminates is seen less clearly. You certainly wouldn't turn off a flashlight if you were trying to make your way in the dark. You'd leave it on constantly. So why "turn off the light" when you putt?

SEEING   **REMEMBERING**

As you focus your eyes and your attention sharply upon the target, you will not be able to think consciously about much else, including the mechanics of the putting stroke itself. That's actually good news, because consciously "thinking your way through" the mechanics of the putting stroke is neither necessary nor desirable. This brings us to the second major explanation of why IP works so well: *the power of athletic intuition.*

As we perform countless activities, from walking to hitting a tennis ball to driving a car, we rely upon a kind of mental ability that is "thoughtless" in the sense that it is devoid of deliberative, conscious thinking. We perform such actions instinctively, automatically, through what we may call "athletic intuition." At the very highest level of athletic performance, pure athletic intuition acts completely unimpeded by conscious thought. As we discussed earlier, a quarterback throwing a football doesn't actually calculate the proper trajectory of the throw or consciously think about how to execute it—he just sees the receiver and sends the ball on its way, instinctively. He relies upon a process that is mental and involves *awareness* of numerous factors, but that is relatively *thoughtless* in the sense of deliberate calculation or conscious control. And the same is true of striking the ball when you are instinct putting. See the target, become aware of as many of the relevant factors as you can, but then execute the putt with a minimum amount of conscious thought about the mechanics of the stroke itself.

You might be surprised at how easy it is to putt instinctively, allowing athletic intuition to control your actions rather than relying on conscious thought. After all, you have probably already learned to do this in other sports. You simply must practice a little to transfer that learning to your putting stroke. For example, you look at the target and not the ball when you throw a baseball, or shoot a basketball, or when you simply roll a ball to a child. Your hands, arms, and shoulders move instinctively to throw or roll the ball to where your eyes tell you it needs to go.

The same thing happens when you putt while looking at the target. With practice, your upper body will instinctively move the putter correctly to send the ball right where you want it to go. Eventually you will no more feel the need to consciously control your actions when putting a golf ball than you would when tossing a football or returning a serve in tennis. Recall our piano analogy in the first chapter. Extending that analogy just a bit, we may now say that the pianist receives a "visual feed of information" from sheets of musical notation, and transforms those figurative notes of ink and paper into audible notes of music by a process that is no more deliberate and no more a matter of conscious thought than throwing a ball or steering an automobile. If the pianist tried "thinking through" the movements of every finger on both hands, the result would be cacophony, not music.

To reach the highest level of skill as an instinct putter, you must mentally transform your putter into a sort of "bionic arm," a fusion of your natural biological arms with the steel-shafted object in your hands. *This point is absolutely important. Club and body must become one.* You normally think of your upper and lower arms as one arm, a single appendage. Now you must think of the putter as just one more part of that appendage. The putter is to your forearm as the forearm is to your upper arm: different parts of one thing. The club is not merely held in your hands, it is unified with them and, through the hands, with your arms and the rest of your upper body.

The putter "feels" the stroke. It responds directly to your brain, through athletic intuition. Of course, you will be aware of the putter throughout the stroke, but in the same way that you were aware of your arm in the Toss Test.

If all of that sounds strange, then consider the catcher's mitt in baseball. Or the racket in the hands of an accomplished tennis player. Driving a car, are you conscious of how far you must turn the wheel to navigate around an object or a pothole in the road? Of course not. You merely look ahead and turn the steering wheel instinctively—you are "instinct steering," in other words. Skillful drivers steer *through* the wheel, not *with* it. It's the same with braking, accelerating, shifting—beginners are clumsy drivers precisely because they have not yet learned the skills of "instinct driving."

"Look at the hole. Trust the stroke." That advice probably still sounds fairly radical, especially to fundamentalists. But athletic intuition is prodigious, resourceful, unerring. Learn to trust it implicitly and you will reach a higher level of skill than you ever imagined possible.

We believe that almost anyone who plays the game of golf can learn to putt competently, if not as brilliantly as Ben Crenshaw or Tiger Woods. And we believe that IP is the way there for many of you. Are you ready to give it a try? Okay, let's get started!

PART TWO

LEARNING INSTINCT PUTTING

Chapter 4

A Refresher Course on the Fundamentals

I'm a believer in fundamentals.

—Jack Nicklaus

Art is thoughtful workmanship.

—W. R. Lethaby

FUNDAMENTALS OF PUTTING

As we said in the Introduction, IP does not require a wholesale rejection of principles that have worked in your own preferred putting style. Having said that, we do nonetheless believe that most golfers would do well to consider a *short* checklist of putting fundamentals. Whether you are a rank beginner or a seasoned player with an eminently serviceable putting style, it always helps to review the most widely accepted principles of grip, setup, and stroke. Consider the following fundamentals, whatever your level of play.

Grip

The most popular putting grip among golfers of all levels is the **reverse overlap grip**, so called because the forefinger of the left hand overlaps the fingers of the right (for a right-handed putter). The palms face each other and the hands ideally fit together to make a single functional unit. While the majority of golfers who use this grip overlap only the forefinger, some choose to overlap two or even three fingers.

Another popular grip is the **ten-finger grip**. As the name implies, all ten fingers are placed on the shaft, with none overlapping. Both hands should hold the putter in the palms, not the fingers. Individual preferences can position the thumbs pointing down the top or side of the shaft. The back of the left hand and palm of the right hand should remain square to the target line (a point to which we'll return in the discussion of alignment).

With either the reverse overlap or the ten-finger grip, we strongly recommend that you have the putterhead square with the palm of the dominant hand, and therefore facing along the target line.

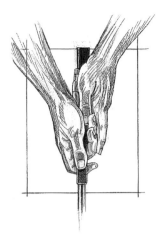

*Traditional reverse overlap
of one finger*

Traditional ten-finger grip

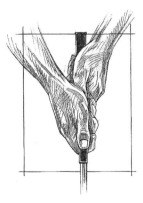

Recall how you "aimed" the ball in the Toss Test. Did you need to "line up" your hand visually in order to send the ball on the intended line? Of course not. We are able to sense—intuitively and very accurately—the directional orientation of the palm of our dominant hand. Thus we can also sense where the putterhead is aimed, even at the precise moment of impact. Directional control is not a problem with IP—as long as you grip the club correctly!

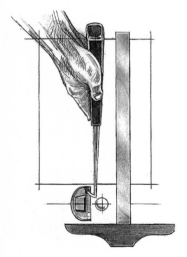

Dominant hand square with putterface

Other grips are less common than the reverse overlap and the ten-finger styles, but they can be just as effective. PGA Tour player Chris DiMarco has done much to popularize the so-called **"claw" grip**. With the "claw," the hands are separated, with the thumb and fingers of the nondominant hand in the conventional position and the fingers of the dominant hand on the top side of the grip. The thumb of the dominant hand is positioned underneath the grip and out of sight. Those who use the claw grip feel that it works well to stabilize the hands, especially when the player feels nervous.

We would mention only one potential problem with the claw grip, and that has to do with directional control. Obviously, the palm of the dominant hand does not point down the target line in the claw grip, as it does in the reverse overlap and ten-finger grips. This "off the line" palm position might compromise directional control, at least for some. However, there is no reason why one cannot learn to sense directional orientation through the fingers of the dominant hand rather than the palm. If you choose to use the claw type of grip, you must discover for yourself how best to sense where the putterhead is aimed. Of course, if you have been using the claw grip for some time and are comfortable with it, you've probably already developed a good sense of where the putter is aimed.

In recent years a number of PGA Tour professionals have adopted the **cross-handed grip** for better wrist stability, particularly on shorter putts. The grip is not actually cross-handed—that is something of a misnomer. This grip places the dominant hand low. In other words, a right-handed golfer would grip the putter with the left hand lower on the shaft than the right hand. While this grip is entirely serviceable, it does present one potential problem for IP. In this case, the directional orientation of the putter is likely to be sensed in reference to the *back* of the dominant hand, not the palm. For some, this might seem less intuitive than sensing direction through the palm of the dominant hand. For others, it might not be a problem at all.

We suggest that you use whatever grip you prefer. And try holding the putter lightly for maximum "feel." On a scale from 0 to 10, with ten as the tightest, try not to get tighter than 5. Hold the club as an infant grasps a person's finger—delicately, yet firmly.

Claw grip

Cross-handed grip

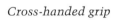

Setup and Alignment

A good setup position is conducive to balance, stability, and comfort. Bend over comfortably from your hips, knees slightly flexed, but don't go into an exaggerated crouch. Let your arms fall into a natural position fairly close to your body, so that your hands swing directly under your shoulders. Position the ball slightly forward in your stance and not too far out from your feet. "Reaching" for the ball is awkward and makes for inconsistent putting. Many golfers prefer a slightly open stance, the better to see the line of the putt. Correct stance and posture have your feet positioned approximately shoulder width with your body weight evenly distributed or slightly favoring the front side, which would be the left side for a right-handed player. Because of the closeness to the ball and the length of the putter, you will be forced to curve your back slightly. Positioning your body comfortably to the ball is the main objective.

Correct alignment has the clubface looking directly at the target—basic physics tells us that the ball *must* go initially in the direction that the putterface is looking at impact. So why not start with the face aimed correctly in the setup? Correct alignment at setup doesn't guarantee correct aim at the moment of impact (see "Mechanics of

Proper stance and setup

the Stroke," page 55), but it certainly increases the odds in your favor.

One of the principal requirements of good shot-making on all full swings is to contact the ball on the "sweet spot" of the clubface. Off-center hits rob you of both power and directional control. The same is true in putting. If you strike the ball off-center, the putter will tend to twist slightly in your hands, which not only dissipates some of the force of the stroke but also sends the ball on the wrong line. Neither distance nor direction will be accurate. When you set up to the ball, always position the putter so that the "sweet spot" is directly behind the center of the ball. The objective in IP is to be able to strike the ball precisely on the sweet spot without looking at the ball as you make the stroke. That might sound difficult, but with careful attention to your setup, and a little practice, it will become virtually automatic.

You might want to find and mark the sweet spot on your putter. Here's how: Hold your putter between the thumb and forefinger of your left hand. Take a golf ball and tap it along the putterface. When you can tap the ball and feel no vibration in the fingers holding the putter, you have found the "sweet spot." It is this spot that should contact the ball.

You might want to mark it with a permanent-ink pen on the top edge of the blade. Then you can see it from the bird's-eye view at address and place it directly behind the ball when you set up to putt. (Many brands of putters feature an identifying spot or line at the sweet spot, but it doesn't hurt to check its accuracy.)

There is one inviolable rule with regard to setting up: *Be consistent.* Remember what we said earlier about the spatial relationship of the golfer to the ball: It must be both *fixed* and *constant.* Find the position that is best for you, and then *force* yourself to assume that position, precisely, every time you address the ball. You must consistently establish the desired relationship of yourself to your putter, and through that, of yourself to the ball at the moment of contact. There is no excuse for being less than perfect in this, the one aspect of execution over which you have 100 percent control. *Never* begin your stroke until you have established the regular geometry of your setup position.

Mechanics of the Stroke

The putting **stroke** differs from the full-shot swing in many obvious respects, all related to the fact that putting requires less distance than hitting full shots does. Putting requires very little movement in the wrists. However, this is not to say that your wrists must be rigid. Rigidity would not be conducive to touch and control. You should strive for a natural, fluid action that is neither stiff nor wristy. Also, there is no need for weight shift or more than the slighest bit of core body motion, due to the lack of distance required. Control of the stroke is left mostly to the arms, whose movement is accommodated by the larger muscles of the back and shoulders. Some very successful putters strike the ball by pulling the club through with the leading arm (the left for a right-handed putter). Most, however, do better controlling the stroke with the dominant arm and hand. As a general rule, do whatever feels most natural to you. In any case, the order of motion begins with the arms and shoulders swinging the club straight back away from the ball, with the clubface staying square to the target line.

At first, the clubhead travels straight back away from the ball with the clubface remaining *square to the target line.* As the backstroke continues, the clubhead travels slightly inside the target line on an arc, with the clubface *square to the arc.* The extent to which the putter moves inside the target line depends on the length of the backswing. Putts of greater distance will generally require a longer backswing, after accounting for slope, grain, and other characteristics of the green.

The forward stroke is essentially a reverse of the backstroke—the putter returns to the ball on approximately the same arc described by the

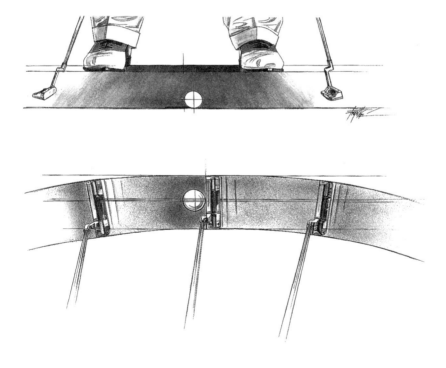

backswing. The clubface must be square with the target line when the putter contacts the ball. Then, after impact, the clubhead continues on the target line briefly before swinging slightly inside the target line again, matching the backstroke in length and relationship to the ground. Throughout the putting stroke your head and body will remain still. After impact you should attempt to hold the finish to review the contact with the ball and to determine if there was excess body motion.

Let's conclude this section on a cautionary note. While it is important to understand the most general principles of good technique, beware the pitfalls of overanalysis. The inventory of specific putting tips, keys, rules, and commandments is virtually limitless: keep a steady head; don't rush the stroke; position your eyes directly over the ball; don't lift your left shoulder; keep the putterhead close to the ground; accelerate through the ball; hold your breath . . . and on and on. All seem reasonable enough, and one or the other tip may be just what the orthodox putter needs to get through those rounds when nothing seems to feel quite right.

The danger in keeping a laundry list of such rules in your head is that they tend to clutter the mind and impede the exercise of athletic intuition. Learn as many putting commandments as you like. Just don't try to remember them all at once! *Above all, do not forget that the skillful instinct putter relies on athletic intuition.* That's why this section on mechanics is relatively brief, compared with most putting books. Orthodox putting is all about delivering the putter to the ball, *mechanically*. Instinct putting is about delivering the ball to the hole, *intuitively*. Practice mechanics deliberately when you're working on correcting a particular flaw, but play with your attention directed at the target, not the stroke itself.

FUNDAMENTALS OF READING A GREEN

Reading a green is as much art as science, if not more. When the chef creates a delicious dish, the product is an artful amalgam of its many elements, something much more than the ingredients in isolation. And such is the art of reading a green. For instance, a putt's speed and its direction are not really separable in practice, because speed affects how much a putt will break. You must always figure in speed when you calculate break. In this sense, all putts that move left or right are also

"speed putts." To make matters even more complicated, the various factors affecting break work together with each other. For instance, the slope
might indicate a left-to-right break, while the grain
would exert a right-to-left influence. Likewise, the
factors affecting speed work together with each
other: Slope increases speed, while wetness re-
duces speed, to mention two important factors. So
remember, the art of reading a green is in weighing
the various factors correctly when you bring them
all together again. The following factors deserve
special attention.

Get an Early Start

The time to begin reading a green is when you're ap-
proaching it from the fairway. The slope of a green is
determined in part by the general lay of the land.
Naturally, you can best see the green in this perspective from a distance. Two familiar "laws" of
putting are sometimes obvious from a long-range
view: The ball tends to move toward water, and slope
usually runs away from mountains.

Architect's Slope

Another characteristic that is sometimes visible
from the fairway, but not once you get to the green,

is what we might call the "architect's slope." An architect will usually build two design features into every green. First, the green must be designed so that it will drain quickly after a heavy rain. Second, the green should be somewhat receptive to a shot. Together, these considerations usually dictate that the green be designed to slope toward the fairway. What this means is that if your approach shot finishes to the left of the hole, the putt will break from left to right, and from right to left if you are right of the hole. Short of the hole, you will have an uphill putt, and finishing beyond the hole will leave a downhill putt.

Fall Line

As you approach the green, try to see its contours, specifically its "spine," or "fall line." A ball that is left of the spine will break from left to right, while a ball on the right of the spine will break from right to left. The farther your ball lies from the fall line, the more it will break, unless, of course, the area to the hole is level. Remember also that putting downhill will increase the amount of break.

If the fall line is not really obvious, you might do well to consider an overall image that Johnny

See the water flow

Miller likes to use: Imagine a giant bucket pouring water down onto the green. Try to visualize where the water would go. Really "see" the water flowing along the putting surface. More often than not, your visualization will be correct.

Go to School

If you missed the green and must play a chip shot, be sure to watch the ball finish. How it moves as it slows will give you a good clue as to the break of your putt. The same is true, of course, for lag putts, both yours and your playing partners'. You should try to "go to school" on every chip and putt.

The Low Down

Many instructors suggest making your first read from behind the ball. Get low to the ground and look along an imaginary line from the ball to the hole. The relatively low viewpoint enables you to see subtle breaks that might not be obvious otherwise. A ground-level perspective also helps you to see the direction in which the grass is growing, the grain.

Grain

Grain affects both break and speed. If the grass is leaning away from the cup toward the ball, the grain is considered to be "against," and it's necessary to hit the putt a little harder than if the grain were toward the hole, or "with." If the grain is right or left with respect to the line of the putt, then obviously it will tend to push the ball in the same direction.

Probably the best way to read grain is simply to look closely at the grass and see which way it is leaning. Also check the edges of the hole. If one side of the hole (the right side, for example) looks brown, with dirt exposed, the grain moves away from the hole in that direction (to the right in this example). Another common method of seeing the grain is to look for dark and shiny areas along the line of the putt. Dark means the grain is against, while shiny indicates the grain is with the line.

Straight Shooting

Some putts obviously move one way or another—the break is very pronounced. Here is a tip that can help when there is very little break. From behind the ball, walk back and forth a few feet to either side of your ball and see if you can find the point from which the putt would appear to be absolutely straight. Sometimes we can sense "straight" better than left or right. As we move constantly back and forth, a sort of visual triangulation occurs that reveals otherwise undetectable undulations in the green. Try it—it works!

When all is said and done, only experience and attention to outcomes will make you a more skillful reader of greens. When you miss a putt, don't just shrug it off and forget it. Ask yourself why.

Naturally, you are eager to get out to the practice green and give IP a try. That is all well and good, but you will get more out of the practice drills if you understand the rationale behind them. So let's talk about some principles of good practice. You just might discover that you've been practicing in ways that don't help your score very much.

Chapter 5

The Principles
of Effective Practice

What I do, I understand.
—Confucius

All practice is *not* created equal. Practice sessions can be productive, or they can be a waste of time—or worse, when you leave the range or green frustrated, confused, and demoralized. The difference all comes down to the conditions under which you practice. If the conditions are appropriate, you will improve. If they are not, you will waste valuable time and your golf skills could actually get worse. In this chapter you will learn about the six conditions that are essential for effective putting practice. Then you will discover what separates really good putters from the rest, a set of characteristics that we call the *Pro's Advantage*. This information will help you to know how much effort to devote to practicing putts of various distances, as well as how hard to stroke your putts.

SIX CONDITIONS OF EFFECTIVE PRACTICE

For practice to be effective, six conditions must be met. You MUST practice (1) when highly motivated; (2) the right things; (3) with a clear-cut purpose; (4) with relevant feedback; (5) the right amount; and (6) the right way. Let's look more closely at each of these essential conditions.

(1) You should practice only when *highly motivated* to improve. The fact that you are reading this book indicates the desire to improve your putting. That underlying desire, that intent, is "motivation," in one sense of the term. And it is a necessary precondition for improvement in any skill or activity. Consider your own handwriting. We write, if only to sign our name, every day of our lives. Has your hand improved, stayed about the same, or become worse since elementary school? If it has stayed about the same or become worse, you probably didn't have the intent to im-

prove. The same principle applies to putting. If the motivation is absent, improvement simply will not happen.

On a different level, "motivation" refers to the enthusiasm and intensity that you bring to practice sessions on a daily basis. Whether due to the demands of work, how rested or tired you feel, or any number of other factors, you are not equally motivated from one day to the next—no one is. When you aren't especially motivated, merely going through the motions will not lead to improvement, no matter how long you keep at it. If you don't really feel the motivation to practice your putting with enthusiasm and intensity, then stay away from the practice green until the motivation is there. And don't worry, it will return.

(2) Motivation alone is not sufficient for improvement. You must practice the *right things*, as well. As obvious as that might seem, many golfers actually waste time practicing the *wrong* things. There are two major objectives on which you should focus. All golfers need to work on distance control—specifically, distance control on putts that contribute most to lowering scores.

Every player has flaws particular to his or her

own putting game. The second thing all golfers should work on is correcting those flaws. Do not confuse flaws with undesirable outcomes. For example, it would be one thing to recognize a tendency to leave putts below the hole, or perhaps too long or short. These are undesirable outcomes. It is quite another thing, however, to know the *root causes* of these problems, the underlying flaws in the mechanics of the stroke. How does one identify those flaws? One could experiment and search for the answers on the practice green without any help, but it would probably be more expedient to take a lesson from a PGA or LPGA teaching professional. The teaching pro will not only identify the flaws causing undesirable outcomes, but also provide the proper correction through appropriate drills and practice goals. This brings us to the third necessary condition for effective practice: having a clear-cut purpose.

(3) These corrective drills and practice goals define the *purpose* of the practice session. You should practice only when you have a clear-cut purpose in mind. For example, your purposes might include proper alignment, better ball position, a smoother stroke, or a steady head position. Any of these pur-

poses might be indicated to correct flaws that cause one to leave putts consistently too far left or right of the hole.

If you have no purpose, you would be better off not practicing at all. Practicing without a purpose merely sets the stage for learning bad habits. You might begin the practice session making good putts, but sooner or later you will produce a few awkward strokes—everyone does. These minor regressions won't bother the focused golfer. But if your practice session is not dedicated to a predetermined purpose, a couple of poor putts will probably lead you to try this, then try that, and then try something else again. Thrash around long enough, and you will eventually find plenty of ways *not* to putt correctly. The undirected mind can be creative, but sometimes in very destructive ways.

(4) Fourth, practice with *relevant feedback* that tells you what you *are* doing when you perform your putting skill as compared to what you *should be* doing. It does little good to know the right things to practice if you don't know whether or not you are performing them correctly when you practice. It may feel right to you, but "how it feels" can be misleading. A popular adage among teaching professionals is, "Feel is not real." Thus, feedback should be as objective as possible.

The best way to receive relevant feedback is to enlist the help of a qualified teacher. Alternatively, you could ask a playing partner to provide feedback; however, a professional will be qualified to offer the most *relevant* feedback. It is also possible to receive feedback from various putting drills and training aids, which your teacher can provide. A video camera can be useful, as can a mirror, especially when it comes to ball position and setup. When all is said and done, one of the very best ways to get relevant feedback is simply to observe the pattern of one's putts. Do inaccuracies consistently appear? What do these outcomes imply?

(5) Fifth, practice the *right amount* for each practice session. How long or how much should you practice per session? There are two major "stop signs" to look for. The first is rather obvious. Stop when you can no longer sustain concentration on the purpose at hand. Beyond that point, you'll simply be going through the motions, and setting the stage to learn bad putting habits. The other "stop

sign" might seem less obvious than the first. *Stop when you are putting well.* That's right; quit while you're ahead! The danger in continuing to practice when you are putting well is that your concentration will flag, which leads in turn to sloppiness, a loss of purpose, and perhaps misguided experimentation. Eventually you'll find a way not to putt so well. Why ruin a perfectly good practice session by going on beyond the point of positive returns?

(6) Finally, it is important to practice the *right way.* There are two types of practice—*skills practice* and *transfer practice.* You must incorporate both to get the most out of your practice routine. Skills practice is appropriate for developing skills, while transfer practice, as the term suggests, facilitates the transfer of those skills to play on the course in competitive situations. Most golfers rely almost exclusively on skills practice, perhaps because they are unaware of the principles or benefits of transfer practice. Both types of practice have a place in learning the methods of IP—and we include some of both in the program we describe later on.

Skills practice is effective for developing specific new skills, or honing previously acquired skills, in isolation from other aspects of the putting game. It operates primarily through repetition. For example, a typical skills development routine would involve hitting a dozen (say) putts from the same distance, with no concern for "playing the ball down." Each ball is putted just one time, the player focusing on a single purpose, such as a smoother stroke, better alignment, or a surer sense of speed. The player would then follow these putts with additional sets, until the skill has been adequately rehearsed. A different set of drills would then focus on a different purpose.

There are times when such practice is appropriate, but it is not an effective way to transfer putting skills from the practice green to the course in actual play. *Transfer practice* is an alternative approach that simulates playing conditions and encourages golfers to practice with competitive situations in mind. After all, the best way to increase your chance of actually playing better is to practice in a way and under conditions that are the same or similar to those you encounter when you play. The greater the similarity between practice and play, the greater the degree of skill transfer.

Transference requires practicing all the parts of the whole putting game together, as they must be performed in actual play. Most golfers rarely, if ever, practice the various putting skills conjointly. How often do you see players using a single ball from various distances, and putting until the ball is in the hole, to simulate actual play? Not very often. But to get better at finishing the hole, one must practice finishing the hole. And do players typically try to simulate the competitive pressure of playing the game by competing with others when they practice putting or around the green to see who can get up and down in the fewest number of strokes? To learn to handle competitive pressure, one must practice dealing with pressure. Get the picture?

As you will soon discover, our practice sessions are designed to engage you in both skill development and transfer training. Yes, there are some purely repetitive drills, especially in the beginning sessions. But as you progress through the program, you will graduate to drills that require you to finish the hole, or "play it all the way down." You will thus practice various skills conjointly. And some of the drills are competitive— either you play against another person, or against yourself in score-keeping exercises.

Practice the right way, and you will not only

develop the skills of IP, but also *transfer* them to the course and competitive play.

THE PRO'S ADVANTAGE

Do you know what separates really good putters from all the rest? We call it the "Pro's Advantage," a set of statistical characteristics that differentiates superior putters from all others. Golf Research Associates (GRA) provides statistical performance analysis for golfers of all handicap levels. (For more information about GRA's analysis programs visit their Web site: www.shotbyshot.com.) Here are some of their findings:

- First of all, they find little difference, among golfers of all levels, from three feet and closer. You are almost as likely as Ben Crenshaw to make those putts that are "inside the leather."

- From ten to twenty feet most golfers two-putt most of the time.

- From farther than fifty feet, almost all golfers are doing well to avoid a three-putt.

- About 95 percent of all lag putts are in the twenty-one-to-fifty-foot range.

In other words, the average golfer putts almost as well as the best golfers in three ranges: three feet and in, ten to twenty feet, and more than fifty feet. The crucial ranges where players at every level tend to differentiate themselves are from four to ten feet, and from twenty-one to fifty feet, the "lag" range. Now consider the following table:

Handicap Level	Percentage of One-Putts	Percentage of Three-Putts
	From 4–10 Feet	From 21–50 Feet
PGA Tour	55%	9%
0–2	50%	10%
3–5	46%	13%
6–9	45%	14%
10–14	41%	20%
15–19	37%	23%
20–24	36%	25%
25–29	35%	29%

Based on GRA data first published in *Golf Magazine* ("Back to Basics," *Golf Magazine*, November 1999).

What do these numbers tell us? Let's compare two golfers, one representing those with handicaps from 0 to 2 (whom we'll call Pro) and the other representing those with handicaps in the 15 to 19 range (Bogey). Pro is more likely to *one-putt* between four and ten feet. And Bogey is more likely to *three-putt* from twenty-one to fifty feet. This latter fact is especially important, given that about 95 percent of all lag putts fall within that range. So, if Bogey wants to putt more like Pro, then Bogey needs to *one-putt more often from four to ten feet, and two-putt more often from twenty-one to fifty feet.* Remember that Bogey is already about as good as Pro from three feet and in, and from outside fifty feet. So these distances are not where most of the difference lies.

Why does Bogey three-putt from twenty-one to fifty feet more often than Pro? The answer is *distance control*—or a lack thereof. According to the SHOT BY SHOT data, approximately 70 percent of all three-putts follow a distance-control error—specifically, failure to get the lag putt within 10 percent of the original distance.

This 10 percent standard is generally consistent with our previous observations. If Bogey could meet the 10 percent standard, a large percentage of his lag putts would finish within about three feet of the hole, from where he putts about as well as Pro. *It cannot be overemphasized that when Bogey three-putts, it is usually because the lag putt is too long or short, not too far left or right of the hole.* Now, remember what the research showed about IP; namely, that lag putts (twenty-eight to thirty-eight feet) finished 24 percent closer than with conventional putting—inside three feet on average. The greatest benefit derived from IP was an enhanced feel for distance. With proper practice you will find this to be true.

While we are on the subject of speed, let's revisit the old debate between "charge" and "die." The "charge" method of putting is to hit the back of the hole hard enough to trap the ball into the cup. The "die" method, by contrast, aims to drop the ball just over the front edge of the hole. Both methods have been used to great success. In fact, two of history's greatest putters used one method or the other: Arnold Palmer was golf's greatest "charge" putter, while Jack Nicklaus was a proponent of the "die" method. Not bad company, those two!

With all due respect to Messrs. Palmer and Nicklaus, one could argue that the best approach lies somewhere in between the extremes of "charge" and "die." Many teachers today advocate hitting the ball firmly enough for it to finish about a foot to eighteen inches beyond the hole if it doesn't go in. There are a couple of reasons why a perfectly struck "die" putt might miss the hole. One has to do with the fact that an area around the hole, some eight to twelve feet in diameter, tends to become somewhat marred with footprints and spike marks. The greater the amount of play, and the longer the hole stays in one location, the greater the number of footprints and spike marks.

Pro one-putts from distances between four and ten feet.

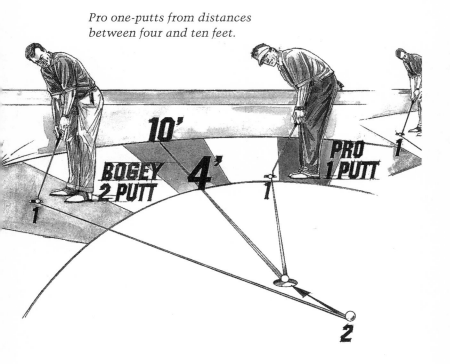

This bumpy area does not extend all the way to the edge of the hole itself, however. The surface just around the cup is typically smooth, because players rarely step there. But it may also be somewhat *raised*, because golfers don't press down the soil in that area, either.

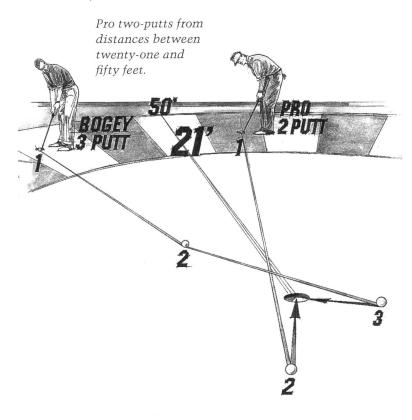

Pro two-putts from distances between twenty-one and fifty feet.

Thus a "die" putt could easily be thrown off-line in the spiked-up area, or veer off its line at the last moment, if the surface is raised just around the hole. On the other hand, the problem with "charging" the hole is that you may find yourself with an unnecessarily lengthy subsequent putt. As we have seen, anything outside of three feet becomes a much more difficult proposition, statistically speaking. The best bet? Hit the putt hard enough to finish about a foot to a foot and a half beyond the hole if it doesn't go in.

The Pro's Advantage yields important implications for practice. Work on one-putting from four to ten feet, and two-putting from twenty-one to fifty feet. Don't spend a lot of time practicing putts shorter than four feet, or longer than fifty feet. And strive for a speed that leaves the ball beyond the hole some twelve to eighteen inches—assuming it doesn't finish in the cup, of course.

So, there you have it—the rationale for all the drills that follow, the "principles of effective practice." We can assure you that understanding these principles will be immensely helpful. You'll know why you're doing the exercises we have selected, and why you're doing them in the order that we suggest. In short, it will all make sense.

To this point we've done a lot of talking about instinct putting, but the closest you've come to actually *doing* it is when you were rolling balls to the hole in the Toss Test. As you probably discovered, it is fairly easy to get the ball close to the hole that way. Unfortunately, the Rules of Golf don't allow this style of "putting" in regulation play. You must stroke the ball with a putter, one of those "weapons singularly ill-designed for the purpose," as Winston Churchill put it in his well-known description of golf. So now it's time to get to work—with putter firmly in hand.

Chapter 6

Getting Started

> We hear and we forget. We see and we
> remember. We do and we learn.
>
> —Old Chinese Proverb

Our purpose is not merely to tell you what IP is. That would be simple enough but ultimately pointless without going beyond words and into action. We want you to be able to *do* IP, to use it on the course and, ultimately, in competitive play. To that end, we have put together a set of drills for you to perform on the practice green. Understand, however, that performing these drills is not an end in itself, as far as we're concerned. We want you ultimately to transfer the skills you learn in practice to play on the course—all to the end of lower numbers on your scorecard.

We have divided these drills into three groups or sets. *You should first read through the material covering all three sets before you begin working on them in practice sessions. After you have familiarized yourself with the lineup of drills, proceed to Chapter 9.* There you will find a suggested plan for success, from stroking those first tentative IP putts on the practice green, to playing competitively with IP on the course. *Begin practicing the drills only after you have read Chapter 9 and have formulated your plan for success.*

But let's not get too far ahead of ourselves. We have a lot of drills to cover before we get to Chapter 9. So let's get back to the business at hand.

The first set of exercises, called Getting Started, will convince your brain that you won't whiff the ball or stub the putter into the ground when you focus your eyes on the target rather than the ball. As happens when you take the training wheels off a bicycle, you will experience a natural degree of uncertainty and lack of confidence about what you are attempting to do for the first time—and fear of the consequences if you should not succeed! These drills will also help you get over the initial awkwardness that always comes with performing an unfamiliar or unpracticed physical skill. In this first set we include: the No-where Drill, the Army Drill, Rapid Fire, the 2×4 Drill, the Inner-Circle Drill, Circle the Hole, and Spot Me.

Recall from the previous chapter that both purpose and feedback are important elements of good practice. To keep these points in mind, we preface each drill by stating its purpose and iden-tifying the relevant feedback.

THE NOWHERE DRILL

Purpose: To strike the ball solidly while looking at the target

Feedback: Observe the roll of the ball; also, try to detect any twisting of the putter in your hands on impact with the ball

To begin to learn to stroke the ball without looking at it, make a number of putts to nowhere in particular. Simply stroke ten successive putts, concentrating only on making a smooth stroke and contacting the ball on the sweet spot of the putter. Don't worry about a target or the distance of the putt. Then retrieve the ten balls and do it again, and again, until you begin to feel comfortable and somewhat confident that you will not mis-hit the ball. After you have performed three or four repetitions of this drill, you will be ready for *the Army Drill,* which introduces a target and begins the process of developing directional control while looking away from the ball.

THE ARMY DRILL: LEFT, RIGHT, LEFT, RIGHT

Purpose: To control the direction of the putter-head at impact; to see the target with both eyes

Feedback: Ball pattern

This drill accomplishes several things. First of all, it further accustoms you to stroking the ball without looking at it. You'll feel awkward and unsure of yourself in the beginning. This drill is a good beginning exercise because the point is not to hole the putt. In fact, it requires you to deliberately miss the hole to the left and then to the right. The second purpose of this drill is to develop some sense of where the putter is aimed throughout the stroke and, most importantly, at the moment of contact with the ball. As you will soon discover, it is not necessary to look at the ball to achieve remarkable directional control. Finally, the Army Drill will teach you to use your eyes in a manner that allows for natural, binocular vision, as opposed to the unnatural monocular (one eye only) perspective that often occurs in orthodox putting.

Place six balls about fifteen feet from the hole. Putt the first ball several feet wide to the left of the hole, and the second ball several feet wide to the right, without looking at the ball as you execute each stroke. Don't worry how far left and right you send those first two balls, but try to narrow the margin with each successive pair of putts. In other words, try to place the second pair of putts inside the first pair, and the final two balls inside the second pair. Don't change your stance or anything about your grip and stroke except where you aim the face of the putter. Do at least two sets of six putts each. With practice you will be able to feel the position and directional orientation of the clubhead with your hands—and you'll gradually begin to trust yourself to contact the ball solidly without looking at it.

Now is also the time to learn how to look properly at the target. In orthodox putting, we nor-

The Army Drill

mally take a couple of final looks at the hole before focusing on the ball and pulling the trigger. The problem is that we don't look at the ball in a natural manner. Rather than looking with our eyes more or less level with the ground, we tend to look "sideways" at the target, with our eyes parallel to the line of the putt, and with our plane of vision more nearly perpendicular to the ground than level. When we do this, we lose the binocular perspective on the target that we rely upon for depth perception. In fact, the nose will sometimes completely block the view of the right eye of a right-handed putter, or the left eye of the left-handed putter. As the Toss Test demonstrates, instinct putting is somewhat similar to bowling. Try bowling a strike with your eyes parallel to the target line! It would not be easy to do. And more to the point, it would not be necessary in order to roll the ball along the correct line to the pins.

This "sideways" manner of viewing an object is actually quite unnatural. Imagine if someone were to shout, just as you were about to putt, "Hey, look! There's a snake in the hole!!" You would immediately look *really intently* at the hole!

And you would naturally turn your head so that your eyes weren't perpendicular to the ground, but roughly *45 degrees to the ground*, as shown in the illustration on page 53.

Do not "open" your shoulders too much or otherwise distort your putting posture. And do not strain to level your eyes. Remain comfortable. You need

Binocular vision provides better depth perception.

to make only a slight adjustment in the orientation of your eyes—justenough to allow a binocular view of the target. You will be surprised at how well you can see both distance and the slope of the green when you properly utilize both eyes.

RAPID FIRE

Purpose: To focus the eyes and attention firmly on the target, away from the ball

Feedback: Ball pattern, number of putts holed

To be successful at instinct putting, you must learn to cast your attention out to the target, away from the ball and the mechanics of the stroke. The Rapid Fire drill trains you to do this by challenging you with the putting equivalent of the turnaround jump shot in basketball. To score the turnaround "J," you must first find the basket with your eyes, then focus your attention on it with laser-like intensity, and then finally send the ball on its way to the hoop—all in about the time it takes to say "hello." Needless to say, there isn't time for a lot of thinking. The shot has to be performed instinctively and intuitively—*with awareness but not deliberation.*

In stark contrast to the turnaround basketball shot, the act of putting is perhaps the most deliberate, unhurried, and studied action in all of sports. Any~~~ ~~~~~~~~~~~~~~~~~
that the prc
terminable
what possibl
"Rapid Fire'
To begin
putting tech
tual play. Tl
your mind t
conscious th ~~~~~~~~~~ ~~~~~~~~~~~~~~~~
letic intuition. When you perform this drill, you simply do not have time to dawdle over the putt, sorting through a laundry list of dos and don'ts.

Here is the drill: Place at least six balls in a

HYDE PARK
PRIME STEAKHOUSE

BOBBY ANDERSON
Executive Chef

716.685.311
Fax 716.685.213
One Walden Galleria P101
Cheektowaga, NY 14225
buffalo@hydeparkgrille.co

Visit Our Other Fine Restaurants At *www.HydeParkRestaurants.co*

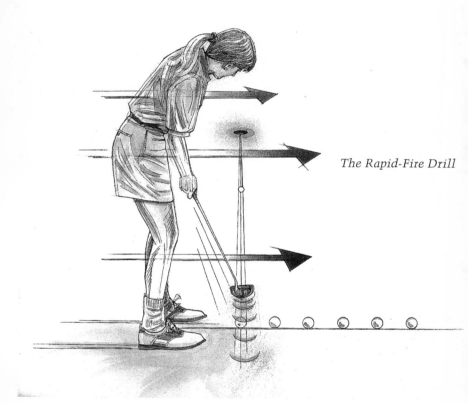

The Rapid-Fire Drill

line, roughly three inches apart, about fifteen feet from the hole. Address the first ball, focus on the hole, and strike the putt. Now, before the first ball reaches the hole, address the second ball and putt it to the hole. Before the second ball reaches the hole, putt the third ball, and so on. Each successive putt must be struck before the previous ball reaches the hole. You will have time for a quick setup and a couple of glances from the ball to the target, but nothing more. No time to think, no time to freeze. As with all putts, pay special attention to distance control. The natural tendency when rushing is to speed up the stroke and contact the ball with too much force, so try to leave the ball no more than eighteen inches beyond the hole.

2 × 4 DRILL

Purpose: To develop a straight back and straight through putting stroke

Feedback: Whether or not the putter touches the boards

The previous three drills dealt with striking the ball, with little concern for mechanics. In this exercise, you'll use two 2×4 boards to assist with the development of a straight back and straight through putting stroke. Place two boards on a level putting surface the width of the putter *plus one inch.* Initially, you should just make practice strokes while attempting to minimize the contact between the toe and heel portion of the putter and the boards. Next, utilizing the same stroke, hit actual putts of varying distance. As before, try to minimize contact between the putter and the boards.

The beauty of this exercise is that you don't have to watch the putter or the ball during the stroke. The boards provide all the feedback necessary. The golfer can look at the target and still know whether or not the stroke is reasonably straight, back and through. This is a great drill to complement the first three, because it helps to instill mechanical skills within the framework—no pun intended—of instinct putting.

THE INNER-CIRCLE DRILL

Purpose: To hole all short putts

Feedback: Number of putts holed; distance beyond the hole when not holed

The Inner Circle will build confidence in your new putting method. This is also a good way to begin and end each practice session and to warm up before the start of a round.

Arrange six balls in a circle around the hole, three feet out from the cup. Putt to the hole, taking care to hit the putts with the proper speed—enough to send the ball about eighteen inches beyond the hole if it doesn't go in. You may vary the lengths of the putts from three feet to four feet out, but stay within that range. From these distances, you should soon be able to sink just about every one of them. Start over from the beginning if you miss. Do several rotations.

When performing this drill you should work on the full cognitive process as well as mechanics. Use your pre-shot routine and activate any thoughts that lead to correct setup, posture, and grip. Then, to get focused mentally on the target, try concentrating on a target that is located at the back edge of the cup. The target could be in the center of the back edge, or slightly left or right of center, depending on the break (which in any case will usually be minimal on putts inside four feet). Stay tightly focused on that target and you'll be amazed at how surely you make those knee-knockers just outside "the leather."

CIRCLE THE HOLE

Purpose: To two-putt from 10–15 feet

Feedback: Number of two-putts

This drill takes the Inner-Circle Drill to the next level of difficulty. In this situation, place ten balls around a single hole at a distance of fifteen feet. Ideally, the putts should vary slightly in break. Starting at the first ball, work your way around the hole, finishing out all of the putts. The point is to two-putt as many balls as possible.

The Army Drill teaches you *how* to look at the target with binocular vision. Before we conclude this section of drills, let us consider the question of *where* to focus your eyes. To say that you should look at the target begs the obvious question, "What is the proper target?" You must look at *something* other than the ball, right? Is it the hole? A spike mark on the green? A blade of grass? An imaginary circle around the hole? Well, for shorter putts that are straight, the target could be a fairly specific spot located at some point around the back of the cup. For putts that break, and for lengthy lag putts, the target might be some spot outside the hole. In any case, the target ought to be as specific as possible, and in most instances that means a spot as opposed to a large area. The reason has to do with the difficulty of learning to direct your attention away from the ball, especially if you are an experienced player and an inveterate orthodox putter. At first you may find it frustratingly difficult *not* to focus on the ball and the putting stroke. "Do not look at the ball" is like being told, "Do not think about pink elephants." Naturally, your mind turns immediately to pink elephants. And so it is in putting. But don't fight yourself. The harder you try not to think about that pink elephant, the more clearly you see it in your mind's eye.

The best way not to think about the ball and your putting stroke (or pink elephants) is to think really hard about something else. And a very good way to do that is to find a specific spot on the green to serve as a target. Offering the mind a *specific* alternative to focus on greatly facilitates redirecting your consciousness away from the ball and stroke. A less specific object, a large or imprecisely defined area, is less effective in focusing the mind, which will tend naturally to return to the ball.

You could take either of two basic approaches to choosing the spot that will serve as your target.

One approach is to pick a spot near the ball on the intended line of the putt. By rolling the ball over that spot, you send it off along the correct path. The other method is to pick a spot closer to the hole. For a couple of reasons, the latter is preferable for IP. First of all, distance control requires that you focus on a point *about* (not necessarily exactly) the same distance away as the hole. A spot just a few inches from the ball, but many feet from the hole, gives little feel for the proper strength of the stroke. The second reason is that a smaller distance from the spot to the ball magnifies the effect of being misaligned. Any error in alignment will be magnified as the spot is chosen closer to the ball and farther from the hole.

These observations suggest that you should choose a mark near to the hole, and as specific as your level of visual acuity will allow. From fifty feet you will not be able to focus on a blade of grass just in front of the hole, unless you have the eyes of a hawk. For lengthy lag putts, a larger area can serve as the "spot," or even an imaginary circle around the hole for those really long putts. For shorter putts, you will do well to fix on a tighter area. And on very short putts, choose a specific target located somewhere on the back lip of the cup. In this situation, distance is really not so important, but making a firm, decisive stroke is. In all cases, remember to stroke the putt hard enough to finish about twelve to eighteen inches beyond the hole if it doesn't go in.

There has been some debate as to whether you should spot putt or, alternatively, "path" putt. We definitely want you to try to envision the putt along its entire length. In this, we agree with those who advocate "path" putting. However, we would argue that the "spot" versus "path" debate presents something of a false dichotomy. After all, how can you choose an appropriate spot unless you also have some idea of the path along which the ball must roll?

SPOT ME

Purpose: To choose, and putt to, a specific place

Feedback: Ball pattern

The Spot Me Drill will help you to think in terms of specific targets. You should perform this drill on a level surface, so that break does not affect the roll. Place four tees in the ground, tightly clustered, about a foot behind the hole. Spot putt to those tees from a distance of four feet. After three putts at this distance, move out two feet farther and do another set of three putts. As you progress out from the hole, you will find it necessary to spread the tees out, in a circle behind the cup, in order to see the target adequately. However, do not enlarge the circle of tees any more than is necessary—let your level of visual comfort be your guide. Continue to lengthen the putts until you reach about twenty feet, and then begin working back to the hole at two-foot intervals. And don't forget: It is better to be slightly long than short.

We close our discussion of this first set of drills with a suggestion that might help when you can't seem to get your attention off the ball and the putting stroke no matter how hard you try. When this happens, return to the Toss Test. Set the putter aside and toss the ball to the target. After you feel that you are refocused on the target rather than your arm or the tossing action itself, then you're ready to return to the drills and try them with the putter.

By now you should be somewhat comfortable striking the ball while looking at the target. The next step is to develop distance control, which will be the subject of our next set of drills.

Chapter 7

Distance Control

> As a general rule, you should always aim for
> the ball to finish past the hole.
>
> —Gary Player

As the title of this chapter implies, this set of drills focuses on that most crucial of putting skills, the ability to control how far you hit the ball. Hitting a large number of putts in succession from the same distance will not help you learn how hard to hit putts from other distances. So in these exercises, you will practice putts of varying lengths.

The drills in this group also begin the process of transfer training, of practicing in a way that will allow you to take the skills you are learning from the practice green to the course. In actual play, you obviously don't have the opportunity to learn by making repetitive putts from the same location. Every putt must be judged correctly the first and only time you attempt it. Similarly, most of the drills in this set involve a single putt from one distance, followed by another putt of a different length, and so on. This second set of drills includes the Semicircle of Trust, Far and Near, the Ladder Drill with a Twist, By the Numbers, and Bull's-Eye.

THE SEMICIRCLE OF TRUST

Purpose: To stroke each putt hard enough to finish approximately twelve to eighteen inches past the hole, if the ball doesn't go in

Feedback: Ball pattern

Remember what we said earlier with regard to "charge," "die," and the proper speed of the putt? *The best speed is that which would carry the ball some twelve to eighteen inches beyond the hole if it did not go in.* With this in mind, place several tees twenty inches behind the hole in a semicircle. Begin at a distance of four feet from the cup and aim at the hole. With each successive putt, progress out at two-foot intervals until you're ten feet away from the hole. Then work your way back in. Try to stroke the putts with enough speed to leave them between the hole and the tees behind it. Strive to make them all, but don't be discouraged if only about half of them go in. As we saw in Chapter 5, Pro's average from this distance is only 50 percent.

Why should the longest putt be only ten feet in length? Well, recall that Bogey and Pro are about equal from inside four feet (both one-putt

The Semicircle of Trust Drill

most of the time), and from inside ten to twenty-one feet (both two-putt). The better golfer's crucial advantage comes in one-putting from four to ten feet and two-putting from twenty-one to fifty feet. The upshot is that Bogey need not worry so much about the ten-to-twenty-one-foot range. We'll get to the longer ranges later on; for now, just concentrate on getting your distance control right from the shorter distances. You'll soon begin to think more in terms of speed, not just direction, when you're within ten feet of the cup.

FAR AND NEAR

Purpose: To leave each putt within a designated distance between two target spots

Feedback: Ball pattern

Golfers who are "line-bound" putters tend to judge distance poorly. The point of this drill is to focus entirely on distance control and not to worry at all about direction or the proper line to the hole. Begin by sticking six tees into the green at three-foot intervals, one tee every three feet. Set up with several balls about fifteen feet from the first tee. To start off, putt the first ball just past the first tee and try to make it stop between the first and second tees. Imagine that the hole is located midway between the tees, but remember: *distance is your only concern here.* You then want to roll the second ball between the second and third tees, and so on. After you're able to do this successfully for each length of putt from closest to farthest, you then need to mix it up. Putt to the last tee, then to the first, then to the third, and so on.

One of the great things about this drill is that once you've mastered it to the point of having each ball stop between the tees, the longest second putt you'll have will be eighteen inches (imagining that the hole is located midway between the tees). You'll be amazed at how good your distance control becomes through practicing this drill. Just make sure you take your mind off the line, because distance is all we're concerned with during this drill.

LADDER DRILL WITH A TWIST

Purpose: Two-putt from a variety of distances

Feedback: Ball pattern; number of two-putts

A variation on Far and Near, this drill begins with the golfer placing tees at five-foot intervals from the hole to a distance of twenty-five feet. First, starting at the shorter distance, work your way out from the hole to the longer distance, trying to two-putt each ball. Next, follow the same procedure, but in this case work from the farthest distance to the shortest. Last, follow the routine in a random order of lengths.

BY THE NUMBERS

Purpose: Two-putt from a variety of distances

Feedback: Ball pattern; calculated performance percentages

This drill is an excellent way to practice both lag putts and makeable short putts. Start with five balls in a circle four feet from the hole. Putt each ball from this distance, but unlike the Inner-Circle Drill, don't start over if you miss. Now place the five balls six feet from the hole and putt them all from there. In this manner, move out to ten feet at two-foot intervals. Calculate your percentage of one-putts. When you achieve 50 percent, you're putting as well as Pro. For example, let's say you made four putts from four feet, three from six feet, two from eight feet, and one from ten feet. Your average is $(4+3+2+1)/20=10/20=0.5$, or 50 percent. Congratulations—you've matched Pro's average.

Next, place five balls in a circle around the hole at twenty feet, and move out to fifty feet at five-foot intervals. This time, calculate your percentage of three-putts. When you get the percentage down to 10 percent, you are as good as Pro. By presenting specific quantitative goals, and a precise way of measuring your progress, this drill allows you to judge your own level of proficiency against the standards of the Pro's Advantage.

BULL'S-EYE

Purpose: Lag putt within 10 percent of the original distance

Feedback: Ball pattern; calculated performance percentages

Another of the important facts comprising the Pro's Advantage is that approximately 70 percent of all three-putts follow a failure to get the lag putt within 10 percent of the original distance. This 10 percent standard means that from twenty feet, for instance, you are likely to three-putt if you are unable to get the ball within two feet of the cup. From thirty feet the lag needs to be within three feet, and so on. Beyond fifty feet, the 10 percent rule puts you more than five feet away, and at that range you must be as good as Pro to get down even half the time. But how many players are "Bogey" from forty feet, yet manage to become "Pro" from four to ten feet? The lesson is clear: if you want to avoid three-putts you need to get those longer lag putts within 10 percent of the original distance.

In this drill, imagine that the cup is the Bull's-Eye on a dartboard and is calibrated with concentric rings at two, three, four, and five feet. Putt three balls from a distance of twenty feet and try to get as close as possible to the Bull's-Eye, as in a game of darts. You may rarely actually hit it, but the realistic goal is to get within the relevant 10 percent ring: the two-foot ring for twenty-foot putts, the three-foot ring from thirty feet, and so on through fifty-footers. Assign values to the rings, just as in a game of darts, and keep score. Repeat the game from thirty, forty, and fifty feet.

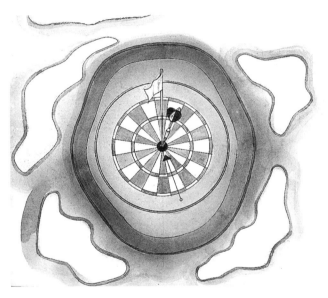

The Bull's-Eye Drill

Chapter 8

Get Real

> The key to faster learning is to use appropriate effort.
>
> —Tony Buzan

This final set of drills takes skill transference a step further with score-keeping and "playing it down" until the ball is in the hole. We encourage you to do these with a playing partner who can serve as a competitor. Of course, you can also do them alone, by keeping score and playing against yourself. The point is to simulate actual play, particularly the pressure of making the lowest possible score. When performing these drills, you should go through the full cognitive process as well—visualizing the putt, activating any pre-swing thoughts that help establish correct address and alignment, and then preparing your mind by clearing any conscious thoughts that might inhibit the free flow of athletic intuition. These drills include: Solitaire, Playing a Round, the Name Game, and Bowling.

Get Real drills are competitive. Bring along a partner and keep score.

SOLITAIRE

Purpose: To play the ball down from various distances chosen at random

Feedback: Number of strokes

This is a great drill to enhance skill transference and to warm-up before play. In this exercise you compete against yourself and keep score for nine or eighteen holes. Simply drop a ball different distances randomly and play the ball down each time. This is very similar to how we play, because our iron shots land different distances from the hole, and we must then putt out. This drill is competitive, but because it does not require a playing partner, it is a convenient drill when you are practicing alone. And because you would bring only one ball to the practice putting green, and could even putt to a single hole, this drill is also convenient if the practice green is congested or if it is small and provides only a few holes.

PLAYING A ROUND

Purpose: To play around the entire practice green, putting the ball down on each hole

Feedback: Number of strokes taken in competition

This one is for practice greens with at least nine holes, and it works best if the green is equipped with numbered flags. The idea is to keep score as you putt around the practice green, playing the ball down at each hole, of course. Think miniature "putt-putt" golf—without the windmill and erupting volcano. The first putt of each hole is taken from a point beside the previous hole. Begin by placing a ball next to hole number one. Putt that ball to hole number two, and play the ball until you hole it. After you've putted out, place the ball next to hole number two and putt to the third hole. Continue in this manner until you finish by putting from the ninth hole back to the first, which is actually the last hole you'll putt in the "round," because number two was the first.

The drill can be done either as medal play or match play, as individual competition or in teams—in short, with all the variations and permutations of competitive golf.

THE NAME GAME

Purpose: Hole any putt designated by your competitor

Feedback: Letters assigned in competition

The Name Game adapts another popular ball game to golf: the basketball-shooting game known as "HORSE." In the basketball version, contestants attempt to duplicate shots that were successfully executed by previous players. For instance, if the first participant makes a twenty-foot bank shot off the backboard, the next player in line to shoot must also attempt a twenty-foot bank shot. Any player who misses is assigned a letter, beginning with "H." When a player misses, the next in the order then attempts a shot of his or her choice, and so on. The object is to avoid picking up letters, and a winner is declared when every other contestant carries all the letters, H through E.

The adaptation to putting is straightforward. Choose a familiar golf name—for example, "Hogan." The first competitor attempts a putt. If it goes into the hole, the others must sink similar putts, or pick up the first letter—in this case, "H."

The Name Game Drill

As with the basketball game, a winner is declared when the others have been assigned all the letters, H-O-G-A-N. For a shorter game, go with a name such as "Wie." If you have all day, "Ballesteros" might be a good choice. The distances ought to be in the four-to-ten-foot range, in keeping with the fact that the ability to one-putt from this range is a crucial advantage that Pro holds over Bogey.

BOWLING

Purpose: Lag putt close to a target ball

Feedback: Ball pattern; points earned in competition

The Bowling Drill borrows from the ancient game of lawn bowling, in which contestants try to roll their balls, or bowls, close to a target ball, called the *jack*. The bowl that finishes nearest the jack scores a point. Bowls are termed *dead* in certain situations, such as when they finish too short or beyond a predetermined limit. An *end* is reached when all bowls have been rolled. Matches may be played for a certain number of ends, usually twelve or fourteen, or until a particular point total is reached. Each participant is given the same number of bowls, typically four in a game of singles.

The Bowling drill adapts lawn bowling to putting. The drill begins with a player rolling the target ball, or jack. Each player putts in turn, and the closest to the jack wins a point. To make this drill more effective, set a limit in front of the ball of 10 percent of the original distance. Thus, any twenty-foot putt that finishes more than two feet short of the jack is dead, even if it's the closest ball. In lawn bowling, a ball that strikes the jack is a *toucher* and earns points no matter where it finishes. Similarly, you could award one or more points to any putt that strikes the target ball. Variations on the basic rules are many. Be creative. This drill is especially effective for intermediate and long putts rather than short ones.

Chapter 9

Your Plan for Success

Progression is unlimited, thank goodness, otherwise golf wouldn't be much fun.
—Johnny Miller

Now that you're familiar with the complete lineup of drills, it's time to think about formulating your plan for success. As with any endeavor to improve—in any department of life—there are some tried-and-true principles one ought to follow. Perhaps the most important principle is to think long-term, but act short-term. That's just another way of saying that one always needs immediate goals in the progression to ultimate goals. Envision the grand prize and be motivated by it. But understand that getting there will happen only by winning a number of smaller victories.

Another principle in formulating a plan for success is to fit your short-term goals to a time-line. The schedule doesn't have to be terribly rigid (after all, golf *is* recreational for most who play the game) but it should be sufficiently disciplined and structured to keep you on track. You'll only be undermining your efforts to learn IP if you try to go too fast, or skip steps in the process. It is rather like climbing a tall ladder. Skipping rungs is an invitation to disaster—and certainly not the surest way to get to the top!

With these principles in mind, we've laid out a fourteen-session plan for success. We strongly urge that you exercise patience and take things one rung at a time. And we do not advise that you try to play with IP on the course immediately. Each phase of the plan involves designated drills to be performed over some number of sessions. These sessions are sequential, but need not fall on consecutive days of the calendar. In other words, the plan does not require you to visit the practice green every day. The weather, not to mention your family, would probably intervene to prevent that from happening, anyway. So let's be realistic and allow for some flexibility in the schedule.

Session 1: The first thing to accomplish is to convince your brain that you won't whiff, or perhaps contact the ball on the heel or toe of the putterface. Begin with the Nowhere Drill. Do quite a few repetitions—putt at least twenty-four balls. Don't try to sink any putts at this point. In fact, you would do well to putt away from any hole—to nowhere in particular, as the name of this drill suggests.

This first experimentation with IP could also involve the Army Drill, if you have the time and your back is willing. Otherwise, save that one for next time. You definitely should not try playing with IP at this point. Continue to use your usual method of putting when you are out there on the course.

Session 2: Begin with ten to twenty putts each with the Nowhere Drill or the Army Drill to warm up and get into the IP mind-set. If you are practicing with a partner, ask him or her to observe your posture, and check to see that your eyes are roughly 45 degrees to the ground, as described earlier.

You should add Rapid Fire to this session. Perform several sets of this drill. Do not be discouraged if you are wildly inaccurate at first. With practice you will improve. Quit when you are able to sink about 25 percent of your putts—or when you start to get tired, whichever comes first. *No playing with IP yet—sorry.*

Sessions 3–5: You could probably dispense with the Nowhere Drill and the Army Drill after a couple of practice sessions, unless you want to use them as a warm-up technique. At this point you ought to do the 2×4 Drill, just to ensure that you're taking the putter back and swinging it forward on a reasonably straight path. It is better to address this potential flaw sooner rather than later. Feedback from the boards is very instructive—no playing partner needed for this one. In fact, you can even set it up at home.

By the fifth session you ought to have progressed to the Inner Circle and Circle the Hole drills. These drills are complementary and can be done together in the same session. Alternate between the two, just to break things up and keep your concentration fresh.

We advise that you not use IP in play on the course yet. But be patient. You're almost there!

Sessions 6–7: Being able to select a target area, particularly of an appropriate size, is really not so difficult on putts inside of about fifteen feet. But beyond that distance, it is. In sessions 6 and 7, you should begin with at least one set of the Inner Circle. Next, do a set of Circle the Hole, followed by Spot Me. Then, alternate between the latter two drills. Stop when you begin to tire, or when you feel that you've made significant progress. Never go beyond the point of positive returns.

Sessions 8–10: So, you've been at it for a whole week's worth of practice sessions—all of the drills in Chapter 6. You are beginning to feel comfortable hitting the ball while looking at the target, and you are even starting to get a handle on direction. Now it's time to start working in earnest on the most important skill in putting—distance control. We cannot overemphasize the fact that *when Bogey three-putts, it is almost always because the lag putt is too long or short, not too far left or right of the hole.* The next few practice sessions should focus almost exclusively on distance control. Take three sessions to go through all of the drills in

Chapter 7 at least one time. Then, if you like some better than others, feel free to concentrate on your favorites. You can now be a bit more flexible in structuring your routine. We went lockstep through the first set of drills, but you can do a bit of picking and choosing from here on. You can also bring a friend along to these sessions—Bull's-Eye and Bowling are great drills for adding a little competitive excitement to your routine.

After a couple of sessions on distance control, you're ready for the day you've been waiting for. It's now time to venture out onto the course with IP. Before your "test-flight" round, pick three holes where you will putt while looking at the target. That's right, *three holes—not eighteen.* And choose the least problematic greens on the course. You are still in a relatively early stage of IP development, and really haven't done much in the way of transfer training. You must not put too much pressure on yourself or your score, which explains why we ask you to limit this first attempt to only three holes. But have faith. You've practiced enough to not whiff or otherwise make a fool of yourself in front of your playing partners.

Speaking of feeling foolish, now is the time for

a brief digression on dealing with the quizzical looks you'll get from your playing partners. Remember, they see you violating the most important principle *they* ever learned about proper putting technique—keeping your eyes on the ball.

First of all, you should think about the results of a golfonline.com (now golf.com) poll conducted by *Golf Magazine*. They asked some 800 golfers this question: *If you knew an odd-looking technique could really improve your game, would you be willing to put up with the giggles and stares of your playing partners?* And how did they respond? Fully 83 percent said yes, while only 17 percent said no. So, where do you see yourself? Are you really willing to believe that eighty-three out of a hundred people are more confident, more self-assured, better able to cope with a little good-natured teasing, than you are? (We didn't think you were.)

Another way to cope with the inevitable skepticism of others is to get a partner to join you in learning IP. There is strength in numbers, after all. But the best way to silence the critics is to beat them on the putting green. Nothing changes minds like success. Before you know it, they'll be flattering you in that most sincere way—imitation.

Sessions 11–14: Continue working on your favorite distance-control drills. And you can continue to use IP in play, if you feel comfortable doing so. It might still be a good idea to limit the number of holes of IP—let your own comfort level be your guide. Understand, however, that you should not really expect to be successful with IP until after you have engaged in several sessions of transfer training. So, beginning with Session 11, you should really shift the focus from skill development to skill transference.

For most of the drills in Chapter 8 you will need a playing partner. Your partner need not be learning IP, of course. In fact, you might challenge a non-IP player to see who can improve the most over some number of sessions. We suggest that you try each of the drills in Chapter 8, and then go back to the ones you enjoy the most. The Name Game and Playing a Round could take longer to complete than some of the others, so time constraints might dictate the choice of drills for a given session.

It is important when performing these skill-transference drills to practice the complete putting routine with each putt. This includes the cognitive process as well—visualization, attention to setup and alignment, and so on. Pretend that you are in a competitive game on the course. Remember, the best way to increase your chance of actually playing better is to practice in a way and under conditions that are the same or similar to those you encounter when you play. *The greater the similarity between practice and play, the greater the degree of skill transfer.*

After fourteen practice sessions you should feel comfortable playing with IP. Go ahead and use IP for as many holes per round as you wish now. But understand that improvement is ongoing. Don't think that you have reached your potential as an instinct putter after just fourteen practice sessions. In reality, you've only just begun to improve. But as Johnny Miller says in the quotation at the beginning of this chapter, improving is what makes golf fun. That, and winning.

Summary and Conclusions

We have covered a lot of ground in this book. It will be helpful to summarize the most essential points in a checklist of sorts. The following are ten essential principles of Instinct Putting.

PRINCIPLE #1: SWEEP OUT YOUR CLUTTERED MIND.

Chances are, you've read or been told countless "rules" of good putting. Most are probably best forgotten. Putting might be difficult, but complicated it is not.

PRINCIPLE #2: STRIVE FOR COMFORT.

When assuming your setup position, avoid extremes, such as crouching over too much or positioning the ball too far out from your feet. A forward position is good, because it promotes a feeling similar to tossing the ball. In general, your body will tell you what is best: If you are balanced comfortably, you are in a good setup position.

PRINCIPLE #3: LET YOUR DOMINANT HAND DOMINATE.

Decide which is your dominant hand and square it to the putter's face. It will be much easier to feel the directional orientation of the putter if you do this. And check your grip with every putt!

PRINCIPLE #4: BE CONSISTENT.

It is imperative that you be consistent in all aspects of the setup position. It is almost impossible to strike the ball consistently on the sweet spot of the putterhead if you constantly vary the spatial relationships, or "geometry," of your setup.

PRINCIPLE #5: REMEMBER THE "TOSS TEST."

Your conceptual approach to IP should be essentially the same as in the Toss Test. Focus on the target, not the ball; be aware of the actions of your arms and dominant hand in much the same way that you are aware of them when tossing the ball to the hole. Go back to the Toss Test whenever things start to go awry with your putting stroke.

PRINCIPLE #6: THINK "DISTANCE."

Distance control is everything in putting. Try to leave the putt just beyond the hole (approximately eighteen inches) if it doesn't go in.

PRINCIPLE #7: PUTT LIKE PRO, NOT BOGEY.

Remember: Pro does two things better than Bogey. He is more likely than Bogey to one-putt from four to ten feet; and he is less likely to three-putt from twenty-one to fifty feet. Keep this in mind when you practice.

PRINCIPLE #8: PRACTICE, PRACTICE, PRACTICE.

In the beginning you will feel very uncomfortable stroking the ball without looking at it. But with repetition you will become familiar with this method and your confidence will grow. When you've practiced enough, your subconscious will begin to take over.

PRINCIPLE #9: BE WILLING TO GET WORSE BEFORE YOU GET BETTER.

While you are learning this new and superior method of putting, your results may temporarily regress. Note the distinction between *method* and *results*. Learn the method. Results are sure to follow in time.

PRINCIPLE # 10: HAVE FUN.

Golf is a *game*. It is to be *played*. Any questions?

We typically acquire a new physical skill in three general stages. First, we present the mind with a thorough understanding of the action to be performed. This is the cognitive stage, and it precedes any actual performance. At this point we are just trying to understand how the putting skill should be performed, so that our mind can instruct our body how to execute it. Second, one trains the body to consciously do that which the mind understands. While we are performing under conscious control, we lack confidence and perform in an awkward, clumsy, and altogether *un*skilled way. But then we practice, over and over again, until our mind progressively develops a better understanding of how to tell the body how to perform the skill more proficiently. With increased practice, our confidence grows, we verbalize less, and our mind gradually gives up more and more conscious control of the movements involved in performing the action—it gets out of its own way, so to speak. Call this the fine-tuning stage of skill development. Third, one moves beyond conscious action and relies upon athletic intuition—the automatic stage. At this level of development you no longer must filter actions through the language portion of the brain. In fact, it will be difficult, if not impossible, to adequately communicate in words "how you do it." Verbal instruction (even to yourself) is of little value at this point. When you perform in the automatic stage of development, your muscles respond directly to the commands of your subconscious mind rather than your conscious thought. And that is where athletic intuition comes into play. The highest level of skill is achieved in this third stage, at which point the best instruction is no instruction at all.

Instruction has nothing to do with ultimate physical skill, for any discussion of technique is irrelevant and pointless in the context of pure athletic intuition. You might as well discuss flight technique with a duck. The point is not that ducks can't talk, but that they would have nothing to say about flying if they could.

And so we arrive at the end of this instructional book. Now it is your turn. We sincerely hope that you will reach that highest stage of skill development. We *know* that you will improve. Now, get out there and put IP to the test.

Acknowledgments

Bob Christina and Eric Alpenfels

Sincere appreciation is extended to the Pinehurst Golf Academy for making it possible for us to conduct the putting research on which this book is based, and to *Golf Magazine* for publishing it. A special thanks is also extended to Lorin Anderson, who encouraged us to conduct the putting research when he was the Managing Editor of Instruction for *Golf Magazine*. And finally, many thanks to two veteran instinct putters, Tony Accetta and John Marentette, who provided us with valuable experiential information about this method from their perspective.

Cary Heath

I am not the only writer in the Heath family. My brother, Merrill, and my cousin, Ellen Heath, are published authors, and I shamelessly imposed upon them for guidance throughout the writing of this book. Thanks, guys. If *Instinct Putting* is deficient in any way, literary or otherwise, it is probably their fault, not mine. Thanks also to A. J. Bonar for his encouragement, and especially for his insistence that we get Phil Franke to do the illustrations. I have pestered Marilyn Allen, literary agent extraordinaire, with far too many e-mails and phone calls, but it's her problem that she will not tell me when enough is enough. Patrick Mulligan has done a fine job as editor, after taking over the project midstream. Finally, I pay tribute to the patience of my family. The children, Will and Alice, gave up cherished computer time while their dad worked on this book. My wife, Lisa, tolerated my irascibility and preoccupation unfailingly. Her love and support sustain me.